HUNGERING

FOR GOD

For He satisfies the longing soul, and the hungry soul he feeds with good things. Psalm 107.9

Rev. Dr. Yvonne I. Ramsay

DEDICATION

This book is dedicated to my spiritual mother **Rev. Helen Watkins Skeetes**; whose relationship with God spurred me on a quest to hunger after God. Thank you, for inspiring me to pant after God for myself.

To my children D'Vonne, Jereme and Jaime Ramsay who have supported me through the years – thank you! I leave you a legacy of faith and prayer.

And to my grandchildren Xavier Levi Timothy Ramsay you are a trail blazer continue to excel. Jamie Madison Ava Ramsay – time will reveal all that you will become.

To every prayer warrior, intercessor and hungry soul who was hungry and thirsty enough to press beyond the prevailing storms of life; those who have stood in the gap in spite of, to seek after the deeper things of God.

Hungering For God by Rev. Dr. Yvonne I. Ramsay

Published by The Bermuda National Library

Edited and Cover Design by Royalwriteragency.com

Copyright © April 2021

All rights reserved. No portion of this book may be reproduced in any form without permission from the publisher, except as permitted by U.S. copyright law. For permissions contact: pastorbreathoflifemin@gmail.com

ISBN: ISBN 978-0-947482-09-1

Printed in United States of America

ACKNOWLEDGMENTS

To every member of Breath of Life Ministries who are living on purpose and have a thirst for the deeper things of God, may you continue to pant after God as He takes us from grace to grace and strength to strength.

To Bishop Neville Smith, Overseer of the International Fellowship of Christian Churches. Thank you for your prayers and continual encouragement and support.

And to those who drop in now and then to refuel or to draw from the waters of salvation; "Blessed are they that hunger and thirst after righteousness for they shall be filled". (Matthew 5:6)

CONTENTS

Dedication I
ACKNOWLEDGMENTS ii
Foreword vii
Preface x
INTRODUCTION xii
Chapter One 1
   Invitation 1
Chapter two 4
   Reflections 4
Chapter three 7
   Experientially 7
chapter four 11
   His presence 11
Chapter Five 13
   Rain of his presence 13
Chapter six 15
   Labor 15
chapter seven 17
   INTIMACY 17
Chapter eight 21
   Come up higher 21
Chapter nine 23

Deep calleth unto deep 23
Chapter ten 25
    push 25
Chapter Eleven 27
    More…. I need more 27
chapter twelve 31
    Believe 31
Chapter thirteen 34
    A test 34
Chapter fourteen 36
    The voice of god 36
Chapter fifteen 39
    Adversity 39
Chapter sixteen 42
    Visions and dreams 42
CHAPTER Seventeen 45
    Ever Green 45
Chapter eighteen 48
    Recovery 48
Chapter nineteen 50
    A knowing 50
Chapter twenty 54
    Waiting Upon the Lord 54
Chapter twenty-one 57
    Show me your glory 57
chapter twenty-TWO 60
    Relentless 60

Chapter twenty-tHREE 63
    Quickly 63
Chapter twenty-FOUR 67
    heart's desire 67
Chapter twenty-fIVE 69
    The Scoop 69
Chapter twenty-SIX 72
    Draw from what you know 72
Chapter twenty-sEVEN 74
    seasons 74
Chapter TWENTY-EIGHT 79
    Life and legacy 79
Chapter twenty-NINE 85
    Obedience 85
Conclusion 89
epilogue 92
Hungering for god 95
Notes 97
ABOUT THE AUTHOR 98

FOREWORD

At a time when there is a cry in the land, a desperation for answers, a temptation to turn to temporary comfort, and seek after several forms of spirituality, it is rare to hear of someone hungering for God. Pastor Yvonne Ramsay is that voice in the wilderness who dares to reawaken a nation to seek after the things of God and reignite a hunger in our hearts for God. In this book, Pastor Ramsay beckons us to draw nigh, enter in and enter a depth in our relationship with Him that will enable us to experience the kind of encounters that will expose us to a newfound freedom and confidence in Him and His word.

Pastor Ramsay is a prophetic intercessor who lives out one of her favorite scriptures "The Lord God has given me the tongue of the learned, that I should know how to speak a word in season to him who is weary. He awakens me morning by morning; He awakens my ear to hear as the learned." Isaiah 50:4

Because of her hunger for God, she walks with a ready tongue, eager to speak a word in season to anyone who is weary. She stands as a vessel, ready to pour into anyone at any time. I have had the honor of being a beneficiary of one whose life Pastor Ramsay has poured into. She has been a treasured spiritual mentor. Having been privy to the mountain and valley seasons of her life, one thing is consistent – a hunger for God. Prayer is not only her daily bread. It is a habit, a lifestyle, a lifeline.

A lifetime of consistent prayer and feasting on the Word has been her food and source of spiritual strength. Many men and women have sat at the table of Pastor Ramsay as she has served them a feast from the word through preaching, teaching, supporting, encouraging, praying, shepherding, and helping them to navigate life's challenges.

In this book, the reader will have the privilege of sitting at the table with her, (symbolically speaking) and have the opportunity to be challenged to be changed, to be provoked to purpose, and be convicted to call out to God as one who is in hot pursuit.

Pastor Ramsay is a like a hidden treasure in the field. Her humility, hunger for God and sincere desire to see souls saved, healed, and set free make her a rare find at a time when it is hard to find authenticity. Pastor Ramsay lives up to the meaning of her name 'Yvonne'; archer as she knows how to hit the target in prayer and through the preached word. The Hebrew meaning of 'Yvonne' is gift of God and Pastor Ramsay is a gift to the world.

If you want to live a comfortable believer's life of status quo, content to eat the crumbs, this may not be the book for you. If you, however, want to join the buffet table and tap into the deep fountain and power that God intended for you, keep turning the pages. Pastor Ramsay provides a wake-up call and opens our eyes to see our spiritual condition. Through the sharing of her stories and application of the word of God, this book will help to create an insatiable appetite for God. If you are hungry and thirsty, even the least bit, for spiritual reality, Jesus invites you, welcomes you, yearns for you to come to the waters and drink up God's presence.

I am eternally grateful to Pastor Ramsay for whetting my appetite over twenty years ago, showing me the deeper things of God. Because of the seeds she has sown in my life, I too have been able to sow into the lives of others. I am only one of many. The multiplication effect of Pastor Ramsay's life will never be known. We do know however, that this is the Kairos time for the world to have this powerful message of revival penetrated in our hearts.

Our hope is not in the odds. Our hope is in God. Our hope is renewed when we hunger for God.

Blessings,

Dr. Crystal Clay

Author, Thrive in True Identity

PREFACE

From a young age I have been inquisitive about spiritual things. In my early teens as a thirteen- year- old I was confirmed in the Anglican Church.

I strived to be good and to do all that I had learned in the confirmation classes I attended for six weeks. It was difficult because I was trying to keep myself. I was not taught in those classes about the Holy Spirit and how He would come alongside me to assist me in living a Christ centered life. This was very frustrating for me. It was around that time I switched churches and began to attend a church where I was taught about having an intimate relationship with God.

It was at that time God placed people in my life that would help me to know Him better; I would be taught about the deeper things of God. These people were not just religious, they spoke of God as if they really knew him. As I listened to the stories of their encounters with God on a personal level, it created a desire in me to want to know God intimately.

Many times when I sit out on my porch relaxing and looking out on the golf course, I would often times end up turning a time of relaxation into prayer. It seemed as if the more I prayed the more I wanted to pray.

This book is a compilation of many encounters I had with God over a long period of time. These encounters have shaped me and influenced my world views on many subjects. Knowing the Bible and knowing God's righteous standard will keep you accountable in these unprecedented times.

Everything has not always been all rosy and bloomy, there have been times of great trials, but my intimate relationship with God has held me steady in the worst of times.

I read a book called 'Beyond the Veil' by Alice Smith. In this book the author speaks of God not having favorites, but He has intimates. That statement has never left me, and it influenced me to want to know God in a greater magnitude.

After many years of serving, God spoke to me at least three times to begin to write of some of the experiences I encountered in my walk with Him. Some things are better caught then taught.

As you desire more of God, He will position people, around you that desire to go higher in Him. The more you grow, it creates a thirst in others for more. A hunger and a thirst for the things of God has brought me to this place. There is so much more that God has that is available to us; *'If we seek, we shall find'* (Matthew 7:7).

You will encounter uphill battles because the enemy of our souls will fight us all the way and it takes a disciplined life to stay the course. God has ordained this book to be written at this particular time for a caliber of people who are thirsty for more.

INTRODUCTION

The Bible says "Blessed are they that hunger and thirst after righteousness for they shall be filled "(Matthew 5:6). When the odds are stacked against you, it is this intense hunger and thirst after righteousness that empowers you to the finish line. This spiritual hunger and thirst are the vehicles that drive your walk with God to the point of fulfillment. 'Hungering for God' is intended to be a transformational reflection of one woman's walk with God over half a century. It has been written because I was given a command from God in my sleep. I accepted the challenge. The purpose of this book is to provoke you the reader to hunger and thirst for more. God always offers us more, but it is up to us to be in hot pursuit of it.

Throughout these pages you will discover my dialogue with God as well as some of my experiences, and how God has led me over these past fifty years. God is a revealer of secrets and he makes himself known to us in so many ways. *'The secret things belong unto the Lord our God but those things that are revealed belong unto to us and to our children forever, that we may do all the words of this law* (Deuteronomy 29:29). What God makes known to us, we become accountable to obey.

Someone may ask, "Do I always experience God as intense as some of these events describe?" The answer is no. God is so awesome He meets each of us at the point of our need in a unique way. However, I have learned to practice being in His presence because God does not always show up in the same way or manner.

The Samaritan woman said to Jesus "Our fathers worshipped on this mountain and you say Jerusalem is the place we ought to worship". Jesus had to make it plain to the woman that, God is a Spirit; and they that worship Him must worship Him in spirit and in truth (John 4:20, 24). We cannot tie God down to a place or a method. The kind of worship that God requires must be in spirit and it must be in truth. Prayer and worship of God unites us in an inimitable way which satisfies the longing of our soul, it also sets us on a course to hunger for more of him. Your trust in God deepens as you walk with him and learn his ways.

In 2001, when I was a student at Briercrest College and Seminary, I had to learn how to balance my studies and my spiritual life so that I would not just be surviving but I would be thriving without lacking in the most important area of my life. Many times, I was overwhelmed with my workload and spent hours at my computer writing papers to meet deadlines and there were times I felt like something was missing because I had known a life of prayer prior to that moment and God had called me to be an intercessor. I knew what it took to bring me to where I was; Experientially, I knew it took years to build a spiritual house and I was adamant that I had to strive to maintain relationship with God and the anointing that God had placed on my life. I recalled the song I had learned in Sunday school as a child, 'Neglect your Bible forget to pray and you'll shrink, shrink, shrink'

One day in Saskatchewan, Canada I was at my computer crying out to God for wisdom while writing a paper and strongly desiring God to feed my hungry spirit at the same time. It was that moment He commissioned me to write a book of short stories "Hungering for God". I wrote a few pages and returned to my studies. A few pages of this manuscript have been in the Archives for nineteen years. All the while I have gleaned much from living life and walking with the Lord. God intentionally allows us to go through different times and seasons that will anchor and steady us; while some experiences provoke us unto good works, others test our faith. There have been many times that my faith has been on trial, but it was only to bring me to my expected end (Jeremiah 29:11b). In hindsight, I have come to understand that God could turn around those tests and use them to work together for my good. I had to learn to let the trials of life work for me, it was important to understand that my suffering wasn't a waste as it was intended to stimulate spiritual growth.

At the tender age of thirteen I read in the book of Genesis that Enoch walked with God (Genesis 5:22). As I read those words, it created a hunger in me to want to know God intimately. I remember saying to the Lord, "If Enoch can walk with you, I want to walk with you". God took me at my word. Life has afforded me journeys through the valleys, foothills of the mountains, and to ascend the mountain peaks. And quite often it has been incredibly challenging to say the least but I had a fervent desire to pursue God at any cost. I would have never made it, if I did not have this hunger and thirst for God. Desiring God is a choice that you can ignore or pursue.

Fifty years later I am still in hot pursuit of the one that is the lover of my soul. *"As the hart panteth after the water brooks, so panteth my soul after thee, O God"* (Psalm 42:1). The enemy is constantly distracting us to take us off course, he wants the attention and praise that belongs to God which is why 'Hungering for God' has to be a daily discipline.

This book 'Hungering for God' is not a prescription but a description of some of my journeying with God. The Holy Spirit commissioned me to put pen to paper to inspire and provoke you to pant after him. If you are hungry for the things of God, may you be provoked to chase the glory.

Psalm 81:10

"I am the Lord thy God, which brought thee out of the land of Egypt: open thy mouth wide, and I will fill it"

CHAPTER ONE

INVITATION

When you are hungry or thirsty you do not wait for an invitation to eat or to drink, you feed yourself and you quench your thirst. We must apply the same principle when it comes to spiritual hunger and thirst for God. One vital requirement for salvation is to recognize your need of God. Once you have a desire to be in right standing with God, He will be found by you. Isaiah appealed to a nation that had turned their backs on God and he invited them to return to God; the only one who can sustain them.

'Ho everyone that thirsteth, come ye to the waters, and he that hath no money; come ye, buy, and eat, yea, come, buy wine and milk without money and without rice. Wherefore do ye spend money for that which is not bread? And your labour for that which satisfieth not? Hearken diligently unto me and eat ye that which is good and let your soul delight itself in fatness' (Isaiah 55:1-2)

When you are in relationship with God you begin to long to be in His presence and the more you partake of His abiding presence the more you thirst after him. The Psalmist David declared, *'O taste and see that the Lord is good; blessed is the man that trusteth in Him* (Psalm 34:8).

When you have confidence in God you position yourself to be blessed by Him and He becomes your comfort and your stay, even when everything around you is chaotic. Knowing God intimately, enables you to rest in the fact of who He is and what He means to you. People that mean a lot to you bring about a calming effect in the midst of a crisis so knowing God becomes to you what the Psalmist David experienced when he wrote, *'He maketh me to lie down in green pastures: He leadeth me beside the still waters. He restoreth my soul; he leadeth me in the paths of righteousness for His name's sake* (Psalm 23:2-3).

The presence of God will bring heaven down to where you are, and prayer will transport you to places you may never physically go because God operates outside of time and space. God can transport you from this physical realm to the spiritual realm and you will see and experience things that otherwise you would not have privy to but by the spirit of God. This kind of relationship disciplines you to begin to commune with God about everything and you feel out of place when you miss your time with him. God really does walk with you and talk with you and He lets you know that you belong to him and He belongs to you. I invite you on a journey of knowing God not only conceptually but experientially. This journey will unveil things you may never have heard of or experienced and it is my desire to create a hunger and thirst in you for more of Him so that you can go in as deep as you want to.

I remember while on a ministry trip laying across a bed in a hotel room, God began to show me very high buildings. He highlighted many different floors and the Holy Spirit revealed to me that when I spiritually outgrow one level or floor I will know when it is time to move to the next level. As time passed, I began to recognize when it was time to shift as I would grow restless and become frustrated at times, because it was time for me to transition. Prayer is never static, there is constant movement and as you discover more of God, you break new ground and ascend to new heights. Thus, you will encounter new experiences.

Ultimately, to have intimacy with God it is essential to have relationship with God. God is closer than our closest breath. You may start by letting God know how much you love and appreciate Him and everything that you are and everything that you have is because of who He is. The more you know God and worship and adore him, the more you will know Him in a personal way.

CHAPTER TWO
REFLECTIONS

Everything has a birthplace or a beginning. I recall very vividly as if it were yesterday, I was sixteen years old and my father died suddenly. My dad was on holiday from his regular job as a prison warden and he woke up and told my mother he had to spend the day with his mother; My paternal grandmother fondly known to me as 'Mama May' lived down the other end of the island. My father left home early and spent the day with his mother and he returned home around 5:00 p.m. in the afternoon on a bus. In half an hour, this bus would leave and travel back to Hamilton. Although my dad was on holiday from his regular job, he did security work at the BELCO plant on Serpentine Road in Pembroke.

He refreshed himself and prepared to catch the bus to go to his security job. I was upstairs and I never went downstairs to see him. I did hear the screen door slam, therefore I stood at the window and was prompted to watch my dad out of sight. I did not open the window to say bye to him, I believe it was because I knew he was pressed for time. I will never forget the urgency I had to watch him out of sight. Later that night I remember my siblings and I in the dining room and suddenly I looked up and saw my dad standing over by his – what we called in those days a pickup. It was a stereo that played 33 or 45 records on a turntable. I did not know anything about visions at the age of sixteen, but I called out to my mother who was upstairs and I asked her why I see my dad standing in the corner even though he is not home. None of my siblings appear to see anything so we carried on with the activities we were doing.

I was awakened very early the next morning because my sister was crying. When I asked her what was wrong she told me she had a headache. I had never seen someone cry that hard from a headache. I persisted in my questioning because her tears were falling profusely, she told me to go with her to the bathroom as our younger sister was asleep in the same room. She closed the door of the bathroom and told me the truth, 'our daddy is dead'. The security man who came to relieve our father of his duties, found dad sitting up in a chair. He stated he was warm as he had not long passed before he arrived. That was not the response I expected. It felt like someone took a hammer and hit me in my head, I now know what I experienced was shock. Within a few minutes of that news the police and Chief prison warden came to our home and delivered the news that changed our lives forever.

I have retold that story because it was my first encounter of having a vision from God. Forty plus years later I was talking to my mother and she stated, I always knew there was something different about you when you told me that you saw your dad standing in the corner of our home when you were sixteen years of age. As I have grown older and reflected on the experience, I have understood it more and more. Samuel was very young when he had a visitation from God. These kinds of experiences prepare us for our calling. Therefore my personal motto I have borrowed from the song, 'A charge to keep have I'.

A charge to keep have I, a God to glorify, a never dying soul to save and fitted for the sky. To serve this present age, my calling to fulfill, and May I all my powers engage to do my Master's will

CHAPTER THREE

EXPERIENTIALLY

I was given a book entitled 'Come away my beloved' by Francis Roberts. This book provoked me and created such a hunger for the things of God. I was in hot pursuit for more. It was not enough to read someone else's experience, I desired to know God on a deeper level and to encounter God for myself. I can relate to Jacob when he encountered God in a dream at Bethel. 'And Jacob awakened out of his sleep, and he said, surely the Lord is in this place; and I knew it not' (Genesis 28:16).

There are visitations from God that are for our illumination, direction, warning, wisdom and assistance. These one- on- one encounters with God are spiritual markers that build our faith and confidence in God. Spiritual Markers move us from one level to another and from one spiritual season to another. When you tap into untapped resources, the word of God and the power of God that is available to every believer, God gives you knowledge of things that otherwise are hidden, it affects the trajectory of your life. 'It is the glory of God to conceal a thing; but the honor of kings is to search out a matter (Proverbs 25:2).

God meets us where we are, He uses the same lingo that we are familiar with. He takes us on journeying that prophetically open our eyes. There are times He has given me insight into past things, present and future events. I thank God for that hunger that not even adversity could diminish. All hell seemed to break loose, because I longed for more of him. I was tested on every level imaginable, yet my love for God did not taper off. Through it all I was fortified and my ministry was birthed out of my relationship with God. I was afflicted but I fought hard not to let my trials affect my relationship with God. I not only survived the onslaughts of the enemy, but God caused me to remain planted by the rivers of water, so that I would bring forth my fruit in my season. It is vital to remain planted by the rivers of water through the afflictions of life. Endurance is key so you do not become uprooted, because you will never produce fruit in your season if you are.

There is a generation of people that need the shade from your branches, and they need the leaves you produce for medicinal purposes. The fruit you produce is vital for their survival, you were created to make a difference in your generation and what God ordains we must maintain. I committed to memory John 15:16 *'Ye have not chosen me, but I have chosen you and ordained you, that ye should go and bring forth fruit, and that your fruit should remain that whatsoever shall ask of the Father in my name, He may give it you'*. Thank God for the sons and daughters that have remained over the years.

I recall waking up one morning and the Holy Spirit spoke to me and told me not to eat any breakfast that he wanted me to fast. He said that He would speak to me on Front Street. I obeyed and by lunch time I had to go on an errand down Front Street, I did not remember the word I was given in the morning. After I entered an establishment and was making a purchase, the salesperson said something unusual as I was filling out some paperwork. I brought my head up and he took me to the side and began to speak into my life. That was the point I recalled that God told me He had something for me. Experiences like this kept me desiring to walk closer with God, all the while I was learning to know the voice of God and not second guess if it was God speaking to me or my own thoughts. Even as I write this, I can hear the spirit of God telling me there is so much more to aspire to. If you desire God, You will find Him and He will lead you and guide you into all truth. In this hour God desires for the church to arise. You cannot live off the fumes of someone else's experience or the fumes of last week's sermon. If you seek him you will find Him when you search for Him with all your heart (Jeremiah 29:13). God desires all of us to come into a closer walk with Him so that he can reveal great and mighty things that we don't even know. Just call unto Him and He will answer (Jeremiah 33:3).

Journeying with God has been one of the most adventurous, satisfying and challenging expeditions of my life. There have been hills to climb and valleys to grow in. I have proven the text, 'The Lord is their strength, and He is the saving strength of His anointed' (Psalm 28:8). Every rung of life has taken me higher, and the higher I climbed, the greater the challenges. God made my feet like hinds feet on slippery slopes; He held me steady and made me sure-footed. Each experience has drawn me closer, made me wiser and enabled me to be able to walk alone. His abiding presence makes up for things that are missing. His presence fills me and has the power to satisfy me.

John 6:35

"And Jesus said unto them, I am the bread of life: he that cometh to me shall never hunger; and he that believeth on me shall never thirst"

CHAPTER FOUR
HIS PRESENCE

I was at my computer one morning working on a paper and I began to cry out to God at the same time. I was caught up in His presence and written below is my experience of my hungering for God.

I saw the heavens open and a pathway of the glory of the Lord raining upon me

I was enveloped into the presence of the Lord and His glory was like a sea about me

God poured out His strength and I was filled with His presence

The floodgates opened wide around me

And I sensed the nearness of the Lord as He circled around me

He invited me into sweet communion with Him

As I entered in, I worshipped Him in the spirit

Allowing His Spirit to fill my spirit

I could see windows in heaven pouring out God's blessings upon me

And my heavenly Father absorbing my worship and praise

I was encouraged to fellowship with Him and He with me

I knew he was pleased, and my soul was satisfied.

After I wrote what is written above, the Holy Spirit said, "not only will you write poetry, but you will write transformational short stories entitled 'Hungering for God'".

CHAPTER FIVE
RAIN OF HIS PRESENCE

As I sought the face of God, I entered a rain forest in a vision. I have never been in a rain forest physically, but God brought me here in a vision. Everything was wet with the presence of God; the water represented the prophetic rain of God. I saw the dew that represented His presence and I saw the mist and the rain drops all around me. I began to dance for I knew I was in the presence of God, all the leaves of the trees were wet. The Lord reminded me that everything that I needed was in His presence. Healing was in his presence, deliverance was in His presence, and encouragement was in His presence; He is Jehovah Jireh my provider. The Lord told me that I had to learn afresh to live in the rain of His presence.

Oh, the water of His presence renewed and revived me. The rain forest was a taste of what it means to live in the overflow. God's continual presence is so tangible, Satan tries to desensitize us, so that we would not feel the presence of the one whose love is ever present. We must always hunger for His presence, and continually seek His face. His presence cannot be taken for granted or substituted, nothing can fulfil the joy and pleasure that He gives. The rain was a reminder of God's unconditional love that is poured out upon us whether we are near or far. Drawing near to the Lord, costs us nothing at all; the only cost was His own son, who died to save us all.

Lord, thank you for the rain of your presence that you promised to send upon all who thirst for you in a dry and thirsty land. In the rain forest I was drenched, I knew not how or when. I just knew I was in your presence which was a God send. You read my heart Lord, and knew I longed to be with you, you permitted me to come up higher filling me with life anew. I came down from the rain forest and I was filled to the rim, not half a cup but an overflow allowing others to drink as I go.

CHAPTER SIX
LABOR

What is written below has not been edited but I have written exactly what was given to me by the Holy Spirit nineteen years ago.

"On October 14th, 2001 I read the scripture from Philippians 3:12-14 while doing my studies and I began to receive revelation. This text caused me to travail in prayer and the Holy Spirit overshadowed me and I labored as I bent over my computer. I began to type with my eyes closed what the Spirit of God was saying to me and allowing me to feel in my own spirit. Thus, these words were penned, I was only the receptacle to receive it.

Father I labor for that which you have placed in my spiritual womb. I do not focus on how you used me yesterday; for yesterday's agenda will not meet the criteria for today. I yield to your Spirit and I submit my spirit to yours even now that I will bring forth the souls that I must travail for today. God, I labor as you give me the vision and the strength to bring them forth. I push forth the young woman that you revealed, God; Usher her in your presence and order her steps, plunge her into a deeper experience with you God.

God is calling the saints of the Most High God, to let go of the past, there is a fresh call today. Jesus gave us one prayer request, *"Pray ye the Lord of the harvest that he send forth laborers into the vineyard"*. (Matthew 9:38). Through prayer you can set my people free; free from worry, free from the oppression of Satan, free from habits, free, free, free! Labor for one purpose; to birth, to bring forth; travail for one reason; to usher in revival an outpouring of my Spirit in this latter day. Press, press, focus on my word, keep your eye on the marker to finish the race; there awaits a prize for you. But you must press forward, heaven's gates will open wide, for the souls that will be set free out of your loins, if you only press. Can you keep pressing when the road is long and dreary, and you can't see your way? When friends disappoint and fail you, can you keep pressing? Listen to the cries of the children and the babies. The young people want to be refreshed, are you willing to be used as my handmaiden? Press. Hell is real, press! Many are in need of your travail, press, press, press; some young woman will not commit fornication if you press in the Spirit on her behalf, press.

I call you to complete and to finish your course, for only those that press toward the mark for the prize of the high calling of God in Christ Jesus will receive this reward. I love you with an everlasting love, as you intercede, I am interceding for you.

The next two paragraphs I have written years later.

Years later I have physically been experiencing spiritual labor pains very intense and they last for many hours or days. I have to travail because it is only through travailing that something is being birthed in the Spirit. My spirit has to come into agreement and declare from my mouth 'Yes Lord' to your will. Sometimes there is such an urgency, so I just yield to the Spirit of the Lord.

'Shall I bring to the birth, and not cause to bring forth? Saith the Lord: shall I cause to bring forth, and shut the womb? Saith thy God (Isaiah 66:9). Just as Israel was going to experience a rebirthing during Christ coming, as we labor in prayer, God will cause us to birth souls and other things He impregnates us with in the spirit. There will be manifestation

CHAPTER SEVEN
INTIMACY

When you hear the word intimacy, it suggests a closeness, togetherness, an attachment or an affinity to an atmosphere, person or thing. Intimacy with God draws you into a closer walk with him and you experience 'Koinonia' which is the translated Greek word for fellowship. Intimacy can lead to intercession because the more you get to know God, the more He reveals His heart to you. Just like a little child sitting in your lap will lean against your chest, and sometimes they will say they can hear your heart going, thump, thump, thump. When we get closer to God, we can hear His heart too. He will entrust us with prayer assignments and woo us into a life of intimacy with Him and begin to reveal His heart for the souls of men. He will lead you into a life of intercession for others; you will begin to hear the cry of God's call as He reveals what is on His heart. God will use you to stand in the gap not only for others but for the nations of this world.

There are times that God would take me to other countries on my knees, I would pray for people in other countries. I recall a time God woke me up around 4:00 am and told me to pray. I laid in my bed praying but He commissioned me to get up and pray. As the spirit of prayer came over me, I had a vision, and I could see a young woman up on a mountain witnessing to a young man. The vision was in technicolor and as she witnessed, I prayed for his salvation. Also, that night I saw a couple at a piano, and I prayed for their marriage. The young woman witnessing to the young man stood out in my spirit and I remember saying to God, 'If I ever saw those people in real life, I believe I would know them. The people that I prayed for, even though I do not have a relationship with them in the natural, there was a spiritual connection that I honored in the spirit to fulfill that which God has entrusted to me.

A couple of years passed since I had those visions, I went on a trip overseas and when I returned, I saw a lady at the church who I had never seen before. The lady came over to me and introduced herself and said she would like to get to know me better. She had invited me on two occasions to have coffee with her after work, each time I forgot and never met with her. The third time she came to my place of employment and left a note. I finally met her at a small restaurant after work, and as we talked, she shared some of her experiences with me regarding her taking Bibles into China. I could sense the presence and power of God as it started from behind and went over my head down to my chin; my eyes became opened and suddenly I knew who she was. She was the girl from my vision years before.

I called her by her name and asked her if three years ago she was somewhere up on a mountain witnessing to a young man. She told me that she had been backpacking up in the mountains and she met a guy and sort to win him for the Lord. I described to her everything that I saw in the vision and how I was interceding, when I was caught up in a vision and encountered them. She told me that night she led the young man to the Lord. I was speechless for a moment, but God brought my words back to me; 'If I ever met the people in my vision, I would know them'. I knew God did this to solidify in my spirit the power of prayer and intercession. After our meeting, within a few weeks she left the island of Bermuda for good. It was an experience I will never forget. The power of prayer will go where we cannot physically travel and accomplish what we can never dream. All these experiences translate into God's faithfulness and how He relates to us personally and individually. God cares for us so much, therefore He continues to unveil himself and show Himself strong on our behalf.

Israel knew God's acts, but Moses knew God's ways (Psalm 103.7). Israel knew God because of the miracles he had wrought on their behalf, but Moses through relationship, learned God's ways. When you know God's ways you do not sweat the small stuff. You do not get stressed over the small things because you know there is a far bigger picture in the larger scheme of things. As we develop intimacy with God, He trusts us with greater and greater assignments. It has been a journey of knowing God and there is still so much more to learn. The Bible admonishes us - 'But grow in grace and in the knowledge of our Lord and Savior Jesus Christ' (2 Peter 3:18). God has always been by my side leading me every step of the way through thick and thin.

During these times of uncertainty God is looking for those who will avail themselves to be used by him. This is a clarion call to the warriors and intercessors that God has need of you. Can you hear the cry of God's call?

Jeremiah 29:13

"And ye shall seek me, and find me, when ye shall search for me with all your heart."

CHAPTER EIGHT
COME UP HIGHER

A new year causes us to recalibrate, refocus and reassess. As I was praying a few days ago, I strongly felt that God was certainly wooing me to higher ground. As I cried out to God by the Spirit of God, I knew that an arrow was being released in the spirit and it hit the intended target. I was encouraged to release arrows of deliverance; Prophetic arrows that would change the trajectory of my life. I knew by the Spirit of God there would be no hit and miss and I remember hearing the word 'elevation'. The spirit of God was calling for me to ascend the stairway that leads to 'higher ground'. I *had to* climb, everything in me knew I had to move and create upward momentum because God takes us higher in degrees; it is step by step, experience after experience. God has so much that He wants to reveal to us, but we must continually 'Come up higher'.

I was definitely in a new season and the very atmosphere or spiritual climate was demanding more of me. There was a churning in my spirit to stay focused and move with expectancy. As I climbed to the higher ground, there were buzzards I had to beat off to press in. I was patiently watching and waiting, like I didn't want to miss anything in that season. I was sensing preparation for what was ahead. So many things have taken place over the years; however, it was at that period I started walking in my 'now'. The oil of the anointing that I received was now flowing and fresh oil was being ministered unto me for that hour and that season.

Truly, it costs something to walk on the high road of surrender. It is a daily surrendering of your flesh and your will to God. Climbing all the way up to higher ground will strip you down to the anointing that is upon your life. When it seems like you have nothing left like the woman in the book of kings. She said all I have is a little bottle of oil. Oil was all that she needed; the anointing is all that you need (2 Kings 4:2). You must be willing to be stripped down so that God can give you what you need; you must be willing to go lower so God can take you higher. I heard a story once of a Pastor that was somewhere in the world up in the mountains. He looked across on a narrow mountain path and he saw two mountain goats. One goat was ascending, and the other goat was descending. As the two goats neared each other on this narrow mountain path, it was obvious that both could not cross. Therefore, they began to charge, this confrontation would cause a process of elimination. Suddenly something unusual happened. The goat that was ascending went down on all fours and the goat that was descending stepped over him. The moral of this story is, 'you must be willing to go lower so that you can go higher'. There are people and things that we must leave behind. When God commissioned Abraham to sacrifice Isaac he had to go up to higher ground and on the way up he had to leave his servants and animals behind and the only things he took was what was required for the sacrifice.

'Come up higher' requires your will, and an act of obedience, as well as a heart that is ripe and ready to experience God in a manner that knows no boundaries.

CHAPTER NINE
DEEP CALLETH UNTO DEEP

The deep place in you calls out to the deepness of God. God has put eternity in our hearts (Ecclesiastes 3:11) and there is a yearning for something more than this world can offer us. We were made in God's image and likeness therefore we need the sweet communion of the Father, there is always a craving for intimacy that can only be filled by Him. That longing cannot be satisfied by anyone else or with anything else. The deep place in you is constantly calling out for more. The psalmist seeks to covey to us his thirst for God. Therefore, he used the hart as a metaphor to describe how deep his desire is for God's presence. *'As the hart panteth after the water brooks, so panteth my soul after thee, O God. My soul thirsteth for God, for the living God; when shall I come and appear before God (Psalm 42.1-2).*

He used the verb 'pant' to express the deepness of his spiritual thirst. He continued to express himself by saying *'Deep calleth unto deep at the noise of thy waterspouts: all thy waves and thy billows are gone over me' (Psalms 42:7).* When life takes its toll on you and you feel like you are in a dry place and separated from God or in despair, use Psalm 42 to quench your thirsty soul. There is a deep place in God that envelopes and circles us in our time of need until we are revived. The imagery he used is like water pouring down into his thirsty soul and going over his head.

I recall a day I had a somewhat heavy heart and I sat at the table to pray and the Holy Spirit said, no need to pray just sit in my presence and let me pour water upon him that is thirsty and floods upon the dry ground. Let me revive you from the inside out. And then I just began to worship, and the more I worshipped the more I was being filled to the overflow. Yes, it was like drinking water on a hot thirsty day, the presence of God began to fill me up. That deep place in God reached over all that was disturbing my peace and sure enough poured a bucket of water deep within me. God knew how thirsty I was and what I needed at that time. *'And the Lord shall guide thee continually, and satisfy thy soul in drought, and make fat thy bones; and thou shalt be like a watered garden, and like a spring of water, whose waters fail not'* (Isaiah 58:11).

I realized that daily I must ask God to quench this thirsting of my soul and fill me up till I overflow. I must keep seeking him so that I will remain sustained by the living water. *'And he shalt be like a tree planted by the rivers of water, that bringeth forth his fruit in his season; his leaf also shall not wither; and whatsoever he doeth shall prosper* (Psalm 1:3).

There will be times you will feel like you are in a dry and thirsty land. Just keep seeking the fountain of living water; that deep place in you can only be filled by the deep place in God.

CHAPTER TEN
PUSH

Many of us are familiar with the acronym 'Push'; it stands for pray until something happens or praise until something happens. When you possess an intimate relationship with God, 'Push" becomes more than an acronym. It will become a part of who you are as you go deep into prayer and lay hold of the horns of the altar and travail in prayer. When you push in the spirit, it involves your whole being and there is a level of travailing that is understood by the spirit alone.

Many years ago, the Holy Spirit taught me that prayer is a place, and I can go in as deep as I want to. I recall someone preaching about prayer years ago and I remember the topic, 'A place called there'. As I have lived some, I began to learn, understand and experience exactly what that topic meant. Prayer can take us to many places, levels, and realms in the spirit. The more you push the deeper you will go to 'A place called there'. And you will know when you get there.

When Jesus took Peter, James and John up on the mountain and He was transfigured before them they wanted to remain. Peter asked if they could stay there indefinitely and build three tabernacles, one for Jesus, one for Moses and one for Elias (Matthew 17:4). Sometimes the glory of God is so tangible we want to stay there, but we do not have the same experience all the time or else it would become too familiar. I used to sit in a chair and pray and experience God's glory, but after a while I could not sense the presence of God like in used in that chair. The Holy Spirit was teaching me not to become familiar with a place or a method of meeting God. For each of us it will be a different experience. God is unique, however one thing is certain 'Blessed are they which do hunger and thirst after righteousness for they shall be filled' (St Matthew 5:6).

There would be times when the spirit of prayer would come upon a person and provoke an urgency to travail in prayer, there would also be times it would be revealed what this deep intercession entails; other times, the purpose might not be revealed until much later. However, when you plough through until you reach a certain place, slowly, the burden lifts from you; that is when you know you have prayed through. One thing is certain we pray until our prayer prevails. It is in prayer that the enemy is overthrown and the purposes, plans and will of God is accomplished in the earth realm.

This kind of pushing involves spirit to spirit. It is the spirit of God that travails through us. *'Likewise, the Spirit also helpeth our infirmities; for we know not what we should pray for as we ought; but the Spirit itself maketh intercession for us with groanings which cannot be uttered* (Romans 8:26).

The Holy Spirit leads, guides and directs us as we push until something happens.

CHAPTER ELEVEN
MORE.... I NEED MORE

In the 80's my spirit was crying out for more of God. Providentially God afforded me the opportunity to attend Morris Cerullo School of Ministry for three months in San Diego, California. There I basked in the halls of spiritual renewal and I learned how to work the works of Christ. It was in this place that I heard God speak to me in an audible voice for the first time.

I was in a prayer room and I was bent over in prayer when I heard the voice of God speak to me telling me to ask him for twins. I looked up to make sure it was not someone else in the room talking to me as the voice was so clear. There was another man in prayer on the other side of the room and he was not even looking at me. I timidly bowed in prayer again and shyly asked God if that was His voice or just my own thoughts. I received an immediate response and He said it was He speaking to me. Then He said, 'do you not know that I give the righteous the desires of their heart?' I had always wanted three children, but because I had been in labor for thirty-six hours with my daughter, I had abandoned the idea of having more children. The Lord continued speaking to me, He told me that if I had twins, I would only be pregnant one more time, but I would also have my heart's desire. I was reminded again by the Spirit of God that He gives the righteous the desires of their hearts and He then challenged me with this statement, 'I will not do it against your will, you must bring your will into alignment with my will'. I thought about it for a few minutes and then I prayed, 'Lord I come into agreement with your will'.

I returned to Bermuda and four months after returning home my husband looked at me and said it would be something if we had twins. I was in shock because I had not shared my experience with him. I questioned why he had made that statement and he confirmed what God had said. The two of us came into agreement with the will of God and the following year (five months later), I became pregnant with twins. I learnt about the deeper things of God at Morris Cerullo's School of Ministry; I went past the point of great blessings from God into a realm of power to do exploits for God. When you have such a longing for more, God will grant your request.

Months after returning to Bermuda, my youngest brother met with a road accident. I was the first to arrive at the hospital out of our family members and the doctor began to tell me how his lungs were punctured, fractured ribs and other complications. As I stood at his bedside in the emergency room, I heard the Holy Spirit say to me "'Take Authority' over every negative word and spirit. Now is time to put into practice what you have learnt". In spite of the grim picture the doctor had painted, I stood my ground on the word of the Lord.

After eight days he was released from the hospital and I was out at the clothesline hanging out laundry. Suddenly the Spirit of God came over me and began to speak to me. The Lord said to me, 'you asked me for a miracle, and I gave you nothing less than a miracle, the death angel had come for your brother, but he was rebuked it in Jesus name'. I was overwhelmed by this revelation from the Holy Spirit and I went into the house to praise the Lord. Within minutes the phone rang, and it was the Youth Leader at our church. She called to tell me the night I told her about my brother's accident, she was in bed and started praying for him. She was given a command by the Spirit of God to get out of bed and travail for him. She said she knew the death angel had come for him and she rebuked it in Jesus name. She stated she could not tell me before, but now that he has been released from the hospital, she was compelled to let me know. Look at the timing of God. Our lives are timed by God, He is in complete control. God had spoken to me minutes before at the clothesline and timed her calling, giving me a confirming word.

This is the power of prophetic intercession, *'And it shall come to pass, that before they call, I will answer; and while they are yet speaking, I will hear* (Isaiah 65:24). *If you have a hunger and thirst for righteousness you shall be filled* (Matthew 5:6). Are you on a quest for more? More of him? He will give you the desires of your heart, you cannot lose by putting God first and everything else shall be added unto you (Matthew 6:33).

Luke 1:37

"For with God nothing shall be impossible"

CHAPTER TWELVE
BELIEVE

God trains us to hear his voice. After I heard the Lord's voice audibly, He would speak to me in many ways. Sometimes it was a strong thought and other times a quiet voice within and other times it would be through dreams and visions.

After my husband and I came into agreement with the will of God as a couple, I thought that was it. However, a further challenge awaited me. Subsequently I heard the Lord's voice yet again, this time the Holy Spirit requested that I prophesy. Prophesy was very new to me at that time. My thoughts of course were known to God and He began to teach me, telling me prophecy was only speaking forth what I heard him say. Now that I was equipped, I was given a command, 'Go and tell people that this time next year you will give birth to twins'; but I was not pregnant at the time I got this command. God revealed to me that there were so many people that doubted He still speaks to people individually. Then I heard the voice of God as a Father lovingly speaking to His child, 'Can I use you to let people know I am still speaking today?

That was enough for me, therefore, I obeyed and began to prophesy that I will give birth to twins that time next year. In spite of the responses I received, I believed God. As I stated in the introduction, this book is not a prescription but a description of how God through the Holy Spirit will be your teacher and school you in the things of the spirit. Things that I knew conceptually, I now know experientially. Once I became pregnant, I prayed every day that the twins would weigh at least five pounds. I did not ask God for the gender of the children, but I knew He gives the best to those that leave the choice to Him. I also prayed continually and daily that I would have the twins quickly. The doctor stated the twins were due September 2nd, but it was possible they would arrive early as it gets crowded in the womb as time progresses. I prophesied in August that I would give birth to twins that time next year. The twins were born August 2nd. The first twin weighed 5lbs 41/2 Oz's and the second 5lb 4 Oz's, they were born after three and a half hours of labor, and they were four minutes apart. God answered every prayer that I had lifted up to him during those eight months of pregnancy. God is able to keep that which you commit unto him (2 Timothy 1:12b).

Every encounter you have with the Lord causes your faith to rise and you begin to recognize the process of living life on purpose, with a purpose and for a purpose. God will use your story to reach a caliber of people that are hungry and thirsty for the deeper things of God; your journey is not only for you, but it is for a crowd of witnesses.

At the tomb of Lazarus Jesus told both Mary and Martha, *'Jesus saith unto her, Said I not unto thee, that, if thou wouldest, believe, thou shouldest see the glory of God?* (St John 11:40).

Your faith is built over time, it is a step-by-step process. Believing is stepping out on nothing and as you step out, God will put something under your feet. May you be provoked to believe God for the miraculous because nothing is impossible for Him and He cannot fail. God will never create a thirst in you to pursue your dreams and aspirations if He does not intend to see it through.

> *Abraham hoped against hope, contrary to hope when it looked like it does not make sense to keep believing. Yet, he held on to the promises of God without wavering. 'Who*

> *against hope believed in hope, that he might become the father of many nations, according to that which was spoken, So shall thy seed be. And being not weak in faith, he considered not his own body now dead, when he was about an hundred years old, neither yet the deadness of Sarah's womb. He staggered not at the promise of God through unbelief; but was strong in faith, giving glory to God; And being fully persuaded that, what He had promised, He was able also to perform* (Romans 4:18-21).

I know this experientially, if God says something He will not go back on His word. It is not in God's nature not to fulfill every word that He has spoken. When God speaks, He will not let one a tiny bit fall to the ground until all be fulfilled. There are times that God has spoken to me that everything around me contradicts what I was told. Even though the odds have been stacked against me I had to continue to believe God; I had to hold on until faith became sight. It is impossible for God to lie, continue to believe God when the facts contradict the truth of what you know about God. You must stand your ground and hold on to what you know. When the angel came to Mary and told her that she would be the mother of the Son of God. Mary's response was *'Be it unto me according to thy word'* (Luke 1:38b).

Our faith only gets stronger as we overcome the tests of life. *'I believe God that it shall be even as He has told me* (Acts 27:25). Just believe! *'So shall my word be that goeth forth out of my mouth; it shall not return unto me void, but it shall accomplish that which I please, and it shall prosper in the thing whereto I sent it* (Isaiah 55:11).

CHAPTER THIRTEEN

A TEST

One evening I was sitting by the fireplace at my home. As I looked at the flames of fire, I reflected on how it has the ability to burn up everything in its path. Whilst I view the ashes below from a few days before, I began to think about what the ashes symbolize. They were residues from the past year yet the flames were so bright and vibrant like a consuming fire. Fire not only consumes but it purges and eradicates everything in us that is not pure.

God tested Abraham and asked him to offer up his only son Isaac as a burnt offering (Genesis 22:1). In the Bible, a burnt offering was completely consumed on the altar. It represented a tribute to God. Abraham faced one of the biggest tests of his life, but he obeyed God. As I meditated on this text, I saw the test that we go through as our burnt offering to God. Our test represents our love, devotion, commitment, and obedience to God. God will never test us above what we are able to bear. Abraham passed the test and God told him, *'Do not slay Isaac for now I know that you fear God because you did not withhold your only son'* (Genesis 22:12). The test was a means to an end. God does not test us to ruffle our feathers, He tests us to prove us. The tests that we go through have purpose.

When I faced one of the biggest tests of my life, I had to hold on to God with every ounce of my being. I had to pray and praise my way through. Abraham had to climb up Mount Moriah to offer Isaac as a burnt offering. For me life became an upward climb and there were days I had to steady myself in prayer so I would make it up the rough side of the mountain. I had to discipline myself to stay focused so that my flesh did not cause me to lose the victory. I had to learn to follow faith over my feelings. Our flesh can blind us to the things of the spirit and tempt us to take matters into our own hands and become defeated. I had to keep my eyes and my mind on God so that the devil did not gain the upper hand. In hindsight I recognize my test was proving my faith. There are times that your faith will be on trial.

My commitment and devotion to God was greater than what I was going through, but it had to be proven. My purpose was greater than the emotional pain I was experiencing and in spite of everything I had to keep holding on. Through tears and heartache, the grace of God was sustaining me.

God provided a ram in the thicket and Abraham offered the ram as a burnt offering in Isaac's stead (Genesis 22:13). God provided the grace I needed to withstand and overcome the test. I would have never made it, if it was not for God's grace and mercy. When God hath tried me, I shall come forth as pure gold (Job 23:10).

CHAPTER FOURTEEN
THE VOICE OF GOD

We must tune in to hear what God is saying for now. God is always ahead of us and He will give us the scoop and keep us ahead of the enemy and danger if we consciously tune in. It is possible to live in the world functioning with our five senses and at the same time listening in the spirit. There are times that God will speak with a still small voice and it is very important as believers that we know the voice of God and obey without hesitation.

Some time ago I was sitting at my computer working and I heard inwardly, get up and go to the next room. Without hesitation I obeyed and went to the next room. As soon as I entered the next room there was a loud crash in the room I had just left and I could not imagine what had happened. The glass light fixture exploded in what seemed a million pieces and it was located almost directly over my head when I was sitting at the computer. I shuddered to imagine what would have happened to me if I had not gotten up immediately from that spot.

Knowing the voice of God can spare your life and keep you from danger. God is concerned about every areas of our lives. There have been times God has instructed me to take my umbrella, take an extra bag, take an extra pair of stockings or go to the cathedral to pray; go to a particular shop or go on a trip or go to the bank – why because all our days are scheduled in a book (Psalm 39:16).

One time I was scheduled to go on a Mediterranean cruise with a group and my British passport did not arrive. The courier company told me my passport was in a bag that was left at JFK airport and would not arrive until the Monday. The group was scheduled to fly out the next evening on a British Airways flight. Someone suggested I remain in Bermuda and catch up with the group as they had a four day stay in Rome before embarking on the cruise. The Holy Spirit instructed me to leave Bermuda with the group and travel with my Bermuda passport and then have someone courier my British passport to me in Rome. I travelled to London on my Bermuda passport and we had a seven-hour layover at Gatwick before taking the flight to Rome. At the airport I saw many clocks and shops that sold watches. One store was called Master of time; God was constantly reminding me that He was in complete control and that He controls time and can tell time what to do. He is not hindered by time, space or even a place. Yes, this was like the acid test, I had to trust him like I always did. This time the enemy was trying to rock me because when I arrived in Rome, I had to present my passport to the authorities.

Before I left Bermuda the Holy Spirit had instructed me that when I get to Rome, I was not to be in the beginning of my group nor at the end of my group, I was to be in the middle. When we landed in Rome, my heart was beating extra fast, but I had to calm my fears with faith. God brought me here to be a testimony and a witness to many of the people that I was travelling with who were unbelievers.

I was getting closer and closer to going up to the booth with my passport. There was one person in front of me when a man went up to the booth of the person who was checking our passports. The Holy Spirit told me to pray that man away from the booth as he would detain me and take me to a room. I began to pray about this, but the man, who I believe was one of authority, was still talking to his employee. I kept praying as I was instructed. When it was my turn, I took my time walking up to the booth and the man I was praying about moved away from booth about that time. I handed over my passport to the person checking passports, and he looked at it as if he knew something was different about it. He looked back at me and then finally waved me on. I wanted to jump for joy, but the Holy Spirit reminded me there were surveillance cameras, so I had to hold in my praise.

We spent four wonderful days in Rome. On the fourth day a coach was coming to pick up the group to take us to the dock to get on the ship. My passport had still not arrived. Everyone was getting on the bus and I was in the lobby of the hotel waiting and waiting. Approximately about 15 minutes before the bus was scheduled to leave, I spotted a DHL courier van across the street at the hotels, and I said this to myself, 'that is the van that has my passport'. I went back to my room to bring down my luggage and when I returned to the lobby, one of the ladies handed me the courier envelope with my British passport. The bus was leaving in three minutes. God never fails. I heard the voice of God telling me to proceed and leave Bermuda without it. Some of the people in the group thought it was risky, but God showed himself strong on my behalf. God was glorified and the people edified. Knowing the voice of God is paramount.

I heard his voice and I obeyed. God will always stand by his word to perform it; For with God nothing shall be impossible (Luke 1:37).

CHAPTER FIFTEEN
ADVERSITY

There was a time I was reflecting on everything I was going through and the Lord gently spoke to me and said "Adversity is not your enemy. How you respond to the trial that comes your way is what will make the difference". Those statements caused me to think and ponder the journey that I was on and I arrived at the conclusion that trial was not designed to take me out; God had a hedge of protection around me. The devil had to get permission from God to tempt Job (Job 1:11).

Your purpose is greater than your circumstances. In a crisis you can still go forward so do not take adversity personally. *The Lord thy God in the midst of thee is mighty, he will save, he will rejoice over thee with joy, he will rest in his love, he will joy over thee with singing* (Zephaniah 3:17). God can break through barriers, and walls will come down on your behalf. It is through prayer that the weak can say that they are strong and the poor in spirit confess they are rich. I had to learn through adversity to see what God sees; I had to push through the pain so I could see beyond the test. That was when I began to redefine adversity and it took on a new meaning. I started to understand that in order for expansion to take place, I had to go through persecution. Private pity parties would sink me lower in despair, therefore I had to learn to encourage myself and begin to see from God's perspective. When I reevaluate where I have been and where I am now standing. I give all the honor, glory and praise to God. My destiny was at stake and I had to fight to keep the end in view.

> *'He maketh me to lie down in green pastures, he leadeth me beside the still waters. He restoreth my soul; he leadeth me in the paths of righteousness for his name's sake. Yea though I walk through the valley of the shadow of death, I will fear no evil; for thou art with me; thy rod and thy staff they comfort me. Thou preparest a table before me in the presence of mine enemies; thou anointest my head with oil; my cup runneth over.*
>
> Psalm 23:2-5

The enemy tried to use adversity to shroud my destiny and use it as a roadblock to stop me from going forward. Thank God for a fighting spirit, I was learning endurance even if I was fighting through tears. I often thought about Nehemiah that rebuilt the walls of Jerusalem with his weapon in one hand and his sword in the other. He was determined the work would not stop and he would not come down from rebuilding the wall (Nehemiah 6:3). Do not allow the enemy to discourage you, at times you may have to take a detour, but ultimately you will reach your destination. No matter what you are going through do not let the enemy steal your hunger and thirst after righteousness, for you shall be filled (Matthew 5:6). If you find yourself wallowing in self-pity, get your fight back and be in hot pursuit of God.

Numbers 12:6

"And He said, Hear now my words; If there be a prophet among you, I the Lord will make myself known unto him in a vision, and will speak unto him in a dream."

CHAPTER SIXTEEN
VISIONS AND DREAMS

God inhabits eternity, yet He is in touch with time, and He chooses to visit His people in various ways. He communicates with us through His word; both the written word and the spoken word. He also uses the vehicle of prayer. Prayer should never be a monologue but a dialogue, as we quiet ourselves before God very often, He will speak to us.

There have been times I have been awakened in the spirit but physically I am asleep. The spirit of God would wake me up and take me somewhere and show me things that He wanted me to know. I recall a time I have been taken way up in the sky and looking down on earth. I was shown a situation that I could see in technicolor, and a message was given to an individual that I could hear; I could also see the person's nonverbal response. A few months later, what I was shown in the spirit became a reality in the earth realm.

There are things that the Holy Spirit would communicate to my spirit while I am praying and sometimes in a vison, He would give me the answer to the things I talked to Him about in prayer; I am speaking of night visions where I could see myself asleep in my bed while I was talking with God. When I awake in the morning the experience was usually very fresh and very real. Other times I would receive a vision while I am awake and praying. God would show me things that He wants me to know that will happen in the future or warnings. Sometimes He showed me these things weeks or months before the events took place in the earth realm.

One night I had a dream about a young man that I did not know much about beyond his name; I also knew his mother. In the dream I saw him with a wife and a baby and he had to make a decision about something. The next day, this young man whom I have not seen for a long time, came to my place of employment. When I saw him, it was surreal as I had just woken up from the dream hours before. I was instructed by the Holy Spirit to tell him the dream after he finished his business transaction. He was literally blown away as he strived to wrap his mind around how I could know such information. He then said to me, 'you must have some kind of gift', but I pointed him to a God that loves and cares for him so much that he wanted to guide him into making the right choice. I was a bit timid to tell him a certain portion of the dream. After he left, I felt convicted as I did not reveal all so I prayed that God would give me another opportunity. The following day I saw him on the street and shared the part of the dream I had concealed from him as it was very serious.

There are a few things the Holy Spirit has given me the scoop, which have not yet manifested on earth. I recall there was a time I had a dream and then I was awakened and told to look at the clock and it was 3:00 am. Twelve hours later (3:00 pm), the dream I had manifested in this natural realm. God forewarns us about some things on many occasions and to be forewarned is to be forearmed. There are many other things that I have seen in the spirit realm before they come to pass in the earth realm. Some of these experiences are a source of encouragement and strength while others give me direction and help me to discern situations. I am encouraged to continue to believe God as I pray because I know it is only a matter of time before there is visible manifestation.

The spirit realm is more dominant than this natural realm, but because we are sensual beings, we are governed by what we hear, see, smell, taste and touch. Our senses keep us connected to the earth realm, but I assure you the spirit realm is greater because what you experience in the spirit takes precedence over things in the earth realm. Many times I find myself in what we describe as 'daydreaming', God communicates things to my spirit that I otherwise would not have known or have privy to. Weeks or months later someone would come and tell me something and I remember God has already told me. At times He would send me places because there are people He wanted me to see; God really does order our steps (Psalm 37:23).

I will instruct thee and teach thee in the way which thou shalt go; I will guide thee with mine eye (Psalm 32:8). God can communicate to us in any way He chooses. *"And he said, Hear now my words: If there be a prophet among you, I the Lord will make myself known unto him in a vision, and will speak unto him in a dream"* (Numbers 11:6). Even as I write, I am challenged to always be in place so that I will be able to hear and to see whether in a dream, a vision or hear the voice of God. Walking close to God is my greatest heart desire.

CHAPTER SEVENTEEN
EVER GREEN

Intimacy with God keeps you sensitive to His voice and whisperings; you become fully aware of the presence of God on a daily basis.

Very recently we experienced a winter hurricane in my homeland, and the velocity of the winds burnt all the hedges, trees and flowers that beautified my property. It looked like we had a fire because of the gale force winds. Everything that was once green and looking very much alive was scorched from the wind. However, there were some trees that added to the landscape which were not affected by the force of the wind. They were still as green as they could be; These trees are classified as evergreens. They were afflicted by the winds but in no way were they affected. As I observed the rich greenness of these trees, I mused besides their ability to endure the elements. There has to be a scientific reason why they experienced the winter hurricane, yet their outward appearance was not affected.

The evergreens were exposed to the same elements like all the other trees, but something about their DNA made the difference. Evergreens remain green; Spring, Summer, Autumn and Winter they do not shed their needles or leaves like other trees. They are unaffected by high winds, storms, hurricanes, and the likes. I began to ponder on why evergreens remained green always. I was learning a spiritual lesson from sitting on my loveseat and looking out the

French doors. God wanted to teach me something, but first I had to understand it naturally, so I consulted google.

> 'The tree's needles contain something called chlorophyll that gives them their
> **green** color. ... It is these sugars that help the tree grow and stay **green**.
> But while some trees, such as maples, stop doing photosynthesis in the
> colder months, **evergreens** keep on photosynthesizing.'

> '**Evergreen trees** don't have to drop their leaves. **Evergreen trees** first
> came from cold climates. ... This shape allows
> the **evergreens** to
> conserve water, which is needed for photosynthesis. Because they
> have more water than their **deciduous** cousins, their leaves stay
> **green**, and stay attached longer.'

The wind blew hard on the evergreen trees and they swayed and leaned from the force of the wind. The storms of life will come, and the winds will blow hard upon us, but if we are anchored in the Lord and remain connected, that is what will make the difference. What we are made out of and what we have stored up along our Christian journey will determine if we remain green and thriving during the winter seasons of our lives. When the winds of life start blowing our way, we will maintain who we are spiritually, mentally, and emotionally. We will not look like what we have been through.

Sometime ago when I spent a lot of time in the secret place, God spoke to me and shared with me this analogy. The time will come when you go through the fire, but you will not be burned. Your hair will not be burnt, and you will not smell like smoke. You will be tried in the fire, but you will come forth as gold. At the time I did not have a clue what that analogy was all about. However, it was just a matter of time. When I look back, it was my relationship with God that kept me in the midst of it all.

Jesus told his disciples, *'In the world ye shall have tribulation but be of good cheer for I have overcome the world'* (John 16:33). We were created to be more than conquerors. *'Nay in all these things we are more than conquerors'* (Romans 8:37). Evergreens were made to endure extreme cold weather. The Spirit of God within us enables us to survive the afflictions and as we live by faith we are not affected by them. Throughout the storms we will remain ever green.

CHAPTER EIGHTEEN
RECOVERY

Recovery can be a slow process, but it does not take away the fact it will happen. Approximately a month has passed since we had the winter storm and all the plants that were burnt from the wind have shed their leaves. Now new leaves were slowly springing forth. Every day it seemed like the leaves tripled overnight. What looked like death was giving way to new life.

As I went for an early morning walk, the new leaves on the hedges and trees caught my attention. As tiny as these leaves were, they appeared alive and vibrant; and in the newness of the day, when everything was still and peaceful, they conveyed a message of hope. It is obvious time is the master teller. If nature is in sync with God to bring forth in its season, that is a lesson worth remembering, and it behooves all of us to surrender the outcome of all things to God. This observance made me conclude that we cannot give up on anything no matter how hopeless the situation appears. We can recover much on our knees in prayer, believing prayer – prayer that moves mountains. Pray always, and even when it is hard to pray, pray anyway.

After David was discharged from going to war with the Philistines against Israel, because they did not want David and his men to join their army, he returned to Ziklag to find all the women and children were taken captive and the city was burned with fire. His men were so overcome with grief, they threatened to stone David. David and his men wept until they had no more strength to weep (1 Samuel 30:1-7). However, David strengthened himself in the Lord and he sought the Lord for direction and the Lord instructed him to pursue the Amalekites for he shall recover all (1 Samuel 30:8).

After the bad weather it appeared that all was lost, and the trees would remain sparse. It really looked as if recovery was not in the near future for weeks. Then slowly what seemed hopeless began to sprout new leaves. Life can be a journey of losses, but God has new things on the horizon. There are things that are ordained to be recovered, and others become a thing of the past. I was encouraged as I celebrated their recovery. I was reminded of the time I fell and fractured my wrist and it had to be set in a cast. It was a painful and a long process and I had to learn to use one hand to do everything. As I adapted to my limitations for a season, I also lived with a forward vision of my recovery. If you are to keep going forward you must keep the end in view.

David recovered all that the Amalekites had carried away and he rescued his two wives and all the women and children the Amalekites took captive and all the spoil. Indeed, David recovered all, nothing was lacking (1 Samuel 30:19).

As we learn to encourage ourselves in the Lord during the difficult times, you too will be strengthened to pursue, for you shall recover all.

CHAPTER NINETEEN
A KNOWING

When something is revealed to you by God, no one, absolutely no one can take it from you. There is a knowing that surpasses earthly knowledge. It is paramount who you share revelations with, as skeptics will try to rationalize what you received by the Spirit. And if you are not wise, you may lose what God intended to make you knowledgeable about.

There are many levels of knowing. We know things conceptually and we know things experientially. For example, there are some things I wake up knowing. If I were asked whether they were dreams or visions, my answer would have been 'No'; God communicates those things to my spirit while I sleep and when I wake up, I just 'know'. It takes place at night while I am sleeping God speaks directly into my spirit. *'The spirit of man is the candle of the Lord, searching all the inward parts of the belly* (Proverbs 20:27). This implies that God speaks to us and guides us through our spirits. You don't always have to be awake when He does that, God can reveal truths to us while we sleep. This kind of knowing can only come from God. I usually take these things and hide them in my heart while I watch and await their fulfilment.

When God reveals things to us, this is a spiritual knowing. You must hold on to it and never release it until it becomes substance. When it enters the earth realm, then it becomes another level of knowing. *'Some trust in chariots, and some in horses; but we will remember the name of the Lord our God* (Psalms 20:7). Trusting God is the key to knowing God and His ways. We learn to trust God through our trials. He enlightens us as we learn the mind of God and He gives us spiritual understanding.

> *'That the God of our Lord Jesus Christ; the Father of glory, may give unto you the spirit of wisdom and revelation in the knowledge of Him: The eyes of your understanding being enlightened; that ye may know what is the hope of His calling and what the riches of the glory of His inheritance in the saints.*

Ephesians 1:17-18

Trusting God is a lifetime experience, and there is always something to learn. It has to be a way of life. The better we know God the more we learn to trust him. If we mediate on God's word day and night, He promised to make our way prosperous, and we will have good success (Joshua 1:9b). Trusting God is not learned overnight, it comes from meditating on God's word. The better you know someone the more you build up trust with that person and overtime you become confident in that individual; therefore, you learn to trust them. But quite often, those people fail us. There is no failure in God. It is impossible for God to fail; therefore, you can trust God with your whole heart.

Knowing God gives you a peace and security. And even when it seems you are walking on thin ice, because you know God, you still trust Him completely. The enemy will strive to rob you of spending quality time with God, so he can keep you anxious about life's woes. He knows that just being in God's presence is empowering. God must be pursued every day, never try to live off your past experiences. Just as God gave the children of Israel fresh manna every morning, He has fresh bread for us every day. *'It is written, Man shall not live by bread alone, but by every word that proceedeth out of the mouth of God* (Matthew 4:4). Knowing God in such a real way makes all the difference even if it is one word you receive from Him. When that one word is a 'Rehma' word, you can live off that word because it is revelation to your spirit. A revelatory word will sustain you during the worst of times.

As you practice having a hunger to hear from God, say to the Lord like little Samuel, *'Speak thy servant heareth* (1Samuel 3:10).

The Apostle Paul was in hot pursuit of knowing God. How bad do you want to know him? To know God is to trust him with your life.

Psalm 27:8

"When thou sadist, Seek ye my face; my heart said unto thee, Thy face, Lord will I seek."

CHAPTER TWENTY
WAITING UPON THE LORD

Have you ever seen an eagle take its flight? Unlike other birds they fly high and when there is a storm they fly above the storm. An eagle's wingspan can be anywhere from seven to nine feet and those wings serve them well. They just don't fly off into the sunset, they fly high. When you are hungry enough for the things of God, you don't have time to hang around with the chickens. You don't spend much time on the ground, you must fly where the eagles fly high about the sky. To attain that kind of altitude you must take time to wait upon the Lord. Your hunger will create a platform for you to seek God and He will teach you how to wait on Him. Quite often your circumstances become the thing that thrust you forward.

Learning to wait on God was birth out of necessity, but after a while it became a discipline. Waiting on God unveils hidden things and enables discovery of hidden treasures. *'Call unto me and I will answer thee and show thee great and mighty things thou knowest not* (Jeremiah 33:3). God is always willing to give us more, because He is the God of more than enough (Genesis 17:1). He takes us from the lesser to the greater, making deposits in us that enrich our lives forever.

Waiting upon the Lord is not always that you are waiting on God for something. Sometimes you have to wait in God. As you wait in God, He starts doing an inward work in you. At times He will become a shelter and a hiding place, He will hide you from the enemy like He did the prophet Elijah; God hid him from Ahab and when it was time God told him to go show himself to Ahab. Privately God will hide you and when it is time, He will reveal you to the nations.

Waiting upon the Lord can also mean you are pausing just to be in his presence. God desires our fellowship; as much as we need Him, He needs us also. Waiting upon the Lord is a time of reflection, meditation and expressing our gratitude for God's faithfulness. One can never truly know the faithfulness of God until you have lived through the unfaithfulness of men.

Waiting on God means dwelling in the secret place of the most high God and abiding under the shadow of the Almighty (Psalm 91:1). This can be likened to when a mother hen gathers her chicks under her wings; they are protected, cared for and supported. On occasion when it is raining, I have seen a mother hen and her baby chicks being sheltered under her wings. This captures the imagery of God and us His children.

Waiting on God is the place where my desire for more is met. *'They that wait upon the Lord shall renew their strength, they shall mount up with wings like an eagle they shall run and not be weary they shall walk and not faint* (Isaiah 40:29-30).

Waiting upon the Lord involves impartation. God imparts so much into us as we bask in His presence. We become the beneficiaries of blessings as we take the time to wait upon the Lord. We are elevated in the spirit, as our strength is renewed. We gain strength to keep going, keep pressing, and keep trusting the one who rewards us just for taking the time to wait. The presence of God can feed a hungry soul; it can nourish you more than natural food and cause you to feel full.

Waiting upon the Lord is transforming on many levels. You never come out of the presence of the Lord the same, He transforms you until you become more like Him in terms of His attributes. As you wait on God to change situations, many times He changes you. It is impossible to remain the same when you have spent time in His presence. You have nothing to lose but everything to gain, because God gave us a promise and that promise is that 'He shall renew your strength. You will mount up with wings like an eagle, you will run and not be weary, and you will walk and not faint'.

As you decrease God will increase in your life. There is a strength that is attainable just from being in His presence. The Psalmist David said, *'My soul wait thou only upon God; for my expectation is from him' (Psalm 62:5)*. David spoke to his soul, not his spirit. It is the soul that hinders us from waiting on God. Therefore, David put his soul in check. He knew where the hindrances lied. The spirit is strong, but the flesh is weak, and it is in the soulish realm that we are distracted mentally and emotionally.

God is the one to teach us how to wait on Him. All He requires of each of us, is to take the time to wait on Him.

CHAPTER TWENTY-ONE
SHOW ME YOUR GLORY

There is a place in God that only seeking souls shall find. The enemy of our souls strives hard to wear us out and wear us down, he wants us to be mediocre and his objective is to render us ineffective and make us complacent. Complacent people are no threat to the enemy.

Many times I have yielded to the Spirit of God and prayed through some days and I usually encourage people to break through and move past surface and familiar prayers in order to go out to where the glory is. I have written without prejudice regarding anyone's prayers; it is human to stick to what we are accustomed to praying. However, there is so much more to aspire to and I have been hungering for His glory.

One particular week as I prayed and waited in His presence, I sensed a shift in the room. The glory of God shifts the atmosphere. As I prayed regarding some particular things, I knew when something in the spirit happened – it was as if a big boulder moved out of the way. I also knew by the spirit that there was going to be a major breakthrough on a corporate level.

The fire of God accompanies the glory of God and is present to bring us to a place where not only is our strength renewed but the essence of who God is, is revealed in all His holiness. One can be anointed of God but not have the fire of God.

Moses had an intimate relationship with God and God spoke to Moses face to face as a man speaks to his friend. The Lord told Moses that the children of Israel are stubborn and He will not go up to the Promised Land with them. However, He would send His angel to go before them (Exodus 33:2); Since Moses was a friend of God and he could not fathom making such a journey without the personal presence of God. Moses pleaded with God to go with him to take the children of Israel up to the land that God had promised to Abraham, Isaac and Jacob. Moses pleaded saying, 'God if you know me by name and if I have found favor in your sight, I need you to go with me or else I am not going'. God relented and told Moses, *"My presence shall go with thee and I will give you rest"*. Moses tapped into God's response and said to God, 'show me your glory' (Exodus 33:17). God again responded to Moses, *'there is a place by me' and I will put you in the cleft of the rock and I will pass by you and cover you with my hands and I will let my goodness pass by you* (Exodus 33:19). Moses did not just want to have conversation with God, he desired to see God's glory.

Believers, we are blessed to know that God is always with us. He told us in His word 'He will never leave us nor forsake us'. Therefore, we have the assurance of His abiding presence. There is a difference between the anointing and the glory. The anointing gives you power to be used by God in the ministry God has called you to, but the glory maintains that level of intimacy. On several occasions after Jesus ministered to the people, He retreated to a solitary place where He had to have fellowship with his Father. We all need that one on one relationship with God.

Praise and worship usher us into His presence but the glory reveals the essence of who God is. This is the place where you experience

God's holiness and all that He is. Moses knew he needed the glory of God.

There are many realms to aspire in God and you will only discover them when you chase after the glory.

CHAPTER TWENTY-TWO
RELENTLESS

Sometimes life will push you to the maximum, but you cannot give up. You must become relentless! That has to be your stance if you are to overcome the pitfalls of life. Relentless faith becomes your theme song in a crisis when you are serious enough to remain above your circumstances and not beneath. You must be determined that no matter how severe the crisis, you will not back down or allow your stance to be weakened; you will stand tall and flat footed and no matter what, keep standing. That is what relentless faith looks like; against all odds you are unyielding.

To be relentless requires faith in God beyond what your circumstances are forecasting. Even when your life does not match your dreams, do not release them. Keep speaking those dreams into the atmosphere, and the power of your tongue will cause your dreams to live. This is what the text in Romans emphasized *'And calleth those things which be not as though they were'* (Romans 4:17).

The church theme that God gave me for 2019 was relentless faith and soon after I received that word, I saw a commercial on television of people who had experienced extreme adversity. And the operative word for that commercial was relentless. God always confirms His word.

I have learned to be relentless in prayer, I cannot back down because of the unique set of circumstances in some instances, but I must be persistent. When I intercede for people that are close to me, I cannot let my emotions get the best of me. The enemy is no respecter of persons and he has no mercy for who you are, his objective is to take you out. *'For we wrestle not against flesh and blood but against principalities, against powers, against the rulers of the darkness of this world, against spiritual wickedness in high places* (Ephesians 6:12). I must stay at it as if my life depends on it. Results come because I refuse to let go or give up.

The whole world has been challenged due to the coronavirus and the scientists have been relentless in searching for a vaccine to combat covid19. I am sure they have worked well above twelve- hour shifts. It will take that same tenacity when it comes to prayer. The Syrophoenician woman was relentless when she sought Jesus out to heal her daughter. Prayer has sustained me through the worst of times, my tears at times were my meat day and night (Psalm 42:3a).

As I was praying one day and pouring out my heart to God, I felt an arm around me comforting me, even though I was alone. I did not open my eyes for I knew it was the comfort of God to get me beyond an emotional point in my life. I had proven God in a way that I had never experienced before. *'Now know I that the Lord saveth his anointed; He will hear him from His holy heaven with the saving strength of his right hand* (Psalm 20:6). During the many years I spent on my lunch hours in the Cathedral in Hamilton praying. It was those prayers which have carried me through and fortified me.

The depth of some experiences is indelible, and they prepare us for what is up ahead. They remain with us always, and when life goes full circle we draw from those experiences. God became my strength when it seemed as if I had no strength left. I look back over those years and I am convinced it was nothing but the hand of the Lord upon me.

You must have a hunger and a thirst for God to keep chasing after Him. The Spirit of God will keep you discerning when the enemy tries to steal your appetite for spiritual things. The enemy will tug at you but *'When the enemy shall come in like a flood, the Spirit of the Lord will lift up a standard against him* (Isaiah 59:19). It was in these unprecedented times that the Spirit of God stirred my heart to share some intimate life changing experiences for others to glean from. In spite of all that was going on in our world, God desires for His people to know and experience him in a very real way. You must remain relentless against all odds. While the enemy may strive to wear you down, letting go and giving up is not an option. Personify relentlessness so that it becomes who you are; someone else needs the strength you receive from God and His word.

As you are persistent in your walk and times spent with God, you are being prepared for destiny's sake. There were times I wondered if my life would ever be normal again, but my fight was not for me alone but for others too. That was the beginning of a life that God was processing to prepare me for the greater call on my life. There were battles to be fought and there were victories to be won! Relentless is who I am and who I must be.

No matter how great the challenge or how hard the trial, I persevere. The lyrics of this song have been a source of strength and encouragement throughout the years.

> *'Never yield a step in the hottest fight, God will send you help from the realms of light; In Jehovah's might put the foe to flight, And the victor's crown you shall wear at last.*

> Charles W. Naylor

CHAPTER TWENTY-THREE
QUICKLY

The world is always moving at a fast pace. In order to keep up with technology we must keep changing and moving. Technology has advanced so quickly we do not need to spend a lot of time waiting for most things anymore; everything is at our fingertips - the push of a button. If things are not happening quickly enough, children of today are bored, because they are so used to having everything moving. Board games are a thing of the past, they must compete with computer games which have sound, and they are fast and moving. Encyclopedias have become obsolete. Everything you want to know is on the internet, just ask Google. Indeed, this is the jet age, the only thing that seems to remain slow are crockpots better known as the slow cooker.

We are predisposed to always be in a hurry because that is the age we are living in. God is never in a hurry! You know why? God revealed to me that He is never in a hurry because everything has a set time or an appointed time to take place. And time only exists under heaven, our God inhabits eternity. In the book of Ecclesiastes, Solomon informs us everything will have its turn in time (Ecclesiastes 3:1). God's quickly and our quickly look totally different. The Bible says in the book of Revelation *'Behold I come quickly'* (Revelation 22:12a). Jesus has not returned as yet, but one thing is certain He is coming soon. God's thoughts and ways are so different from ours. *'For my thoughts are not your thoughts, neither are your ways my ways saith the Lord* (Isaiah 55:11).

As I was in prayer the Holy Spirit spoke to me about the word quickly. 'When God moves suddenly, quickly will feel like it has always been'. You can be waiting for something for so long, and then suddenly it happens and you get so caught up in that moment of time that you forget how long you have been waiting for it. A Kairos moment can happen suddenly and then it feels like it has always been.

It is similar to an expectant mother; her gestation period is nine months. Then one day her due day arrives and suddenly she goes into labor. The labor is hard, and her travail seems endless, all she wants is to deliver a healthy baby and get on with life. The process can wear the mother down; the pregnancy was one thing, but the delivery is quite another. The mother desires the birth to be quick, but most times giving birth may be several long hours of labor. Once the mother delivers the baby and she is able to hold the newborn in her arms, immediately she forgets the long period of labor for her baby has been born. Time is swallowed up in the joy of the birth. Quickly and suddenly to God represent 'A moment in time', 'an appointed time'. Our perception of quickly is when the delay is over.

I was praying one time and I heard a sound in the spirit 'whoosh, whoosh!' I asked God, 'what was that?' and He told me that what He has for me in eternity was being released in time. at that point, it was impressed upon my spirit that no matter how long I have to wait for something, I must not move or be moved because what God has for me is waiting for me in eternity and when eternity releases the thing into time, if I am not in my place, I will not receive it.

God is the one that teaches us how to wait. We learn how to wait in prayer and trust God to complete what he started in us. Even though 'quickly' looks different from God's perspective, don't become weary. Let your faith outlive your wait. Anything worth having is worth the wait.

God will not go back on his word! Therefore, continue to expect a move of God suddenly!

Proverbs 25:2

"It is the glory of God to conceal a thing; but the honor of kings is to search out a matter."

CHAPTER TWENTY-FOUR
HEART'S DESIRE

We all have longings and desires that we learn to bury deep within us under lock and key. Sometimes we release them to others, or we keep them close to our hearts. Every now and then they emerge, and we feel them tugging at our heart strings. These desires are things that only God can fulfill. They appear to be beyond our reach, but they are not unattainable. We have things that are dear to our hearts and we like to keep them tucked away from public view. Sometimes those secret desires get the best of us and we wear our hearts on our sleeves. I recently heard someone on television say it like this, 'A letter from the heart can be read on the face'.

Our God is intimately familiar with us and knows our thoughts afar of. He knows our down sitting and our uprising, our going out and our coming in (Psalm 139:2). There is nothing about us that is hidden from Him. In order for those hidden things within us to be fulfilled, God tells us what to do in order to allow them to manifest. *'Delight yourself in the Lord and He will give you the desires of your heart* (Psalm 37:4). This happens when you find all your joy and pleasure in His will. Make him your delight, and your desires will be in His will.

God really does give us our heart's desire. I have experienced a time in prayer that God stirred me to ask Him for a particular thing. As I pondered the request, the Holy Spirit spoke directly to my spirit with these words, "Do you not know that I give the righteous the desires of their heart". The Holy Spirit continued speaking to me telling me, He will not do it against my will. I must bring my will into alignment with His will'. After a few minutes of thinking things over, I responded by saying, 'I will bring my will into alignment with your will. And Father whatever your will is for my life, grant it as I am in agreement with your word.'

There is pleasure in knowing God and doing His will. It is a sense of being full and satisfied when you have done the will of the Father. As we delight ourselves in God, He delights Himself in us. It gives God pleasure to see His children walking in agreement with His plans for their lives. Just like an earthly father is pleased with His children, so God is pleased with us and He delights in our obedience to His will.

Delighting ourselves in the Lord has everything to do with our will being in sync with the will of the Father. God granted me my heart's desire because it was in alignment with His will.

I shall never forget the lesson I learned in prayer that day; when God's will becomes our will – what a joy and fulfillment filled my soul.

CHAPTER TWENTY-FIVE
THE SCOOP

Human nature likes to be in 'the know'. People are inclined to want to know things. I want to know all I can about God. I discovered that knowing more about God affected my surviving and my thriving. It does not matter if everyone else is going down stream, I must go up stream against all odds. Revelation from God gives me enduring power and I am able to see beyond what I see with my natural eye.

When we call on God, He sure enough answers. He may not send the answer when you want him to, but He answers in His time. As I reflect over the years of asking God to reveal truth in matters that humanly I could not make sense of, He always gave me a revelation. Once I was awakened during the wee hours of the morning and the Holy Spirit instructed me to look at the clock and it was 3:00 a.m. The Holy Spirit instructed me to pray and target a particular thing as I engaged in spiritual warfare, pulling down things that would exalt itself against the knowledge of the truth. I was shown a vision and it was very clear what I had seen. Twelve hours later the thing that I had been shown manifested in the earth realm and God gave me an answer. Once again, I was instructed to look at the clock and it was 3:00 p.m.

Whenever I experience these kinds of phenomena, I coined them God giving me the scoop. Another word for 'scoop' is 'revelation'. If we would only take time to call on God! The enemy wants to keep us in the dark, but what Satan tries to conceal from us, God will reveal. It is vital to embrace the word of God and believe what it declares. *'Call unto me and I will answer thee and show thee great and mighty things that thou knowest not'* (Jeremiah 33:3). God will always keep us ten, twenty, thirty or fifty steps ahead of the enemy. It is so important that we seek the face of God because it is during those times of seeking His face He removes the veil and shows us hidden things.

I recall being very tired on a lunch hour at work. I went to a secluded place to eat lunch and I said, 'Lord I am so tired'. He told me to go to sleep but first He said look at the clock. I dozed off to sleep and I had a vision, it was not a dream. The difference was I had on the same clothes I really had on and I was in the same place. A little girl touched me and said 'three years'. I had the opportunity to look at the little girl, but I was so caught up with what she was saying I did not look at her features.

I woke up and pondered over the vision; it felt like hours but only five minutes had passed. Time does not exist in the spirit realm, only on earth. However, I was still tired, so the Holy Spirit told me to go back to sleep. I was awakened by the sound of the most beautiful bells I have ever heard, never have I heard such a beautiful sound. The Holy Spirit woke me up and let me go; it was 1:00 p.m. and it was time to go back to work. What an experience! Years later, I was on the floor praying and the Lord said to me, that little girl that you saw in the vision she was – and He gave me her name. The next day after I had that experience, someone came to my place of employment and gave me a book. They told me the Holy Ghost instructed them to give it to me. The book was called, 'How we can know one another in the spirit'. I had the vision and then God sent the book to me.

I was reminded of the date and the year I had the vison and the Lord told me the date the child was born. It was exactly three years from the date I had the vision. I asked the Holy Spirit what it was about, and He told me that she was announcing her birth. When her parents were expecting, I always had an affinity to the baby in the mother's womb and I did not know why at that time. The Holy Spirit even told me they would ask me to be her godmother and I was to say yes because it was of Him. God certainly reveals things to us that otherwise we would not have privy to. God does reveal secrets, and He chooses when to reveal them to us.

CHAPTER TWENTY-SIX
DRAW FROM WHAT YOU KNOW

When life gets tough as it sometimes will, and you are between a rock and a hard place, you must draw from what you know. You need discernment to hold on to a God given vision when everything around you is changing and your dreams do not match your reality; You must hold on to what you know. What do you know about God? What has God brought you through when it looked impossible? In order to survive the pitfalls of life you must draw from what God has done for you in the past.

When Saul wanted to put his armor on David, David told Saul he cannot wear his armor because he had not proven it (1 Samuel 17:39). David relied on what he knew. He used his shepherd's sling and five smooth stones in fighting Goliath (1 Samuel 17:40). In times of great testing, I had to rely on what I knew about God and the areas I had proven Him for myself. It is not in God's character to lie or go back on His word; it is impossible for God to lie. Therefore, pull to your remembrance what you know about God.

I constantly remind myself of God's unfailing love and His faithfulness. His promises are yea and amen (2 Corinthians 1:20). Sometimes God will use nature to remind me of what I know about Him. He used my Easter Lily plants that were about four inches in height and were in the embryonic stage of their development. I was watering my plants and I suddenly smelt a strong scent of Easter lilies. God knows how much I love to smell lilies. The lilies have a very strong smell when they are in full bloom. There were no flowers on the plants as yet and they had just started to sprout little buds- little buds that would become lilies in time. Therefore, I questioned God as to what this occurrence meant. The Holy Spirit whispered to my spirit, "I am going to do just what I said".

The lilies may not be visible to your natural eye yet, but they have the potential to become lilies in time. It was just a matter of time. I was reminded of the scripture, *'Be still and know that I am God, I will be exalted among the heathen, I will be exalted in the earth'* (Psalm 46:10). I had to pause and remind myself of what I know about God. This experience was a source of encouragement to my soul. That year I had more lilies than I have ever had. God will use the plant kingdom, the animal kingdom or anything to get my attention. Whatever God ordains to be, will be.

CHAPTER TWENTY-SEVEN
SEASONS

Time cannot stop your season, the only person that can stop your season is you. If you allow the woes of life to get the best of you, it will keep you stuck in a season of grief and pity. Consider natural seasons, they do not come to stay they eventually come to an end. You are the only one that can make a conscious decision to rise up out of the ashes of despair and despondency and move forward.

Even the prophet Samuel was grieved because God had rejected Saul from reigning over Israel. And the Lord asked the prophet Samuel a question, 'How long will you mourn for Saul, seeing I have rejected him? (1 Samuel 16:1). Samuel could have missed the next season of David's life because he was grieving over the past. God had to shift gears in Samuel's life so that he could move forward. God was not against Samuel grieving, but his grieving was prolonged, that was why He asked the question, 'how long will you mourn for Saul'. When our grieving prevents us from living - that is when God will intervene.

The Syrophoenician woman's faith brought time forward. Jesus told her *'it is not meet to take the children's bread and feed it to the dog'* (Mark 7:27b). It appeared that Jesus was pushing the woman away, but Jesus was only building her faith. The woman was not offended, she did not run away, but rather the woman pushed back. She responded to Jesus by saying, *'even the dogs eat the crumbs that fall from the Master's table'* (Mark 7:28). She pushed back so hard that Jesus brought her future into her present, her tomorrow became her today.

Your faith can bring your future into your present. Don't let offences stop you from pushing back. Time did not stop the Syrophoenician woman's season, and it will not stop your season. What season are you in? Is it a dry season, a season of pain, a season of delay, a season of disappointment or disillusion? Perhaps it is a waiting season; a waiting for marriage season, a season of redemption, an expectant season, a season of surprises or a season of anticipation.

Have you ever experienced a prolonged season and it seemed endless? There have been times I had visitations from God using people and circumstances to sustain me. I was at a crossroad one time and there were several people waiting on the other side to cross as well. One of the people was an old grey- haired man I had never seen before. The Holy Spirit told me when you get in the middle of the street make eye contact with the man. As soon as I heard that the light went off and everyone started crossing, as I came close to the man, I looked him in his eyes. And he said to me very forcibly 'the Lord has a blessing for you'. As I reached the other side the man continued on his way and never looked back.

Another time I caught a taxi, and the driver was someone I have never seen before, he engaged me in conversation and by the time I reached my destination, he said, 'God has a blessing for you!'. There was still something I had to do; I had to maintain my praise and worship to stay fueled so I could keep going forward.

Whatever season you are in, know that God controls times and seasons, and He can redeem time. If you are in a prolonged season and you are ready to quit, I encourage you to keep holding on to the horns of the altar, God knows where you are. Keep praying through, God will reveal Himself and the process will get easier as you discover God's ways. When you know that God has visited you and He has revealed certain things to you, you can be certain He will not go back on His word. Therefore, do not waste your season because it is working for you. You must have enough faith and confidence to prophesy over yourself and declare the word of the Lord. Insist that you are not going anywhere because your season will come.

If you have sown seeds, then you will reap a harvest. Prayer is a seed, fasting is a seed, sowing is a seed and quality time spent with God is a seed. And a seed has the ability to transmit life. Every seed that you have invested will bring a return.

God has a word for every season that you are in, and God gives us grace for the season. Therefore, forget about giving up because you can't take it anymore. Quitting is never an option and it is God's grace that has kept you so far. God will give you a word for every season to sustain you. If He can provide flesh for the prophet through a raven, God will feed you spiritually through the seasons of life and He will sustain you to make the journey to your next season. One day God revealed to me that I must expect things from unexpected places. Sure enough, blessings began to come from places that I least expected. God has some surprises for you, and they shall come to pass at the appointed time.

In prayer God prepares us for the next chapter and season of our lives. When you have a prayer life and walk closely with God, He will not hide things from you. In Genesis 18, God says 'shall I hide from Abraham that I am going to destroy Sodom and Gomorrah because of the wickedness of the city?' When God revealed His plans to Abraham, Abraham interceded for the city because his nephew Lot and his family were there. Lot and his family were spared because God revealed His judgment on the cities to Abraham who had a covenant relationship with God.

May your hunger and thirst for God increase as you pant after more of Him. He has a place for each one of us by Him. Find your place, no one else can position themselves in your designated spot. As much as we long for God, God also longs for us to dwell in His presence. There is no substitute for the presence of God. As we desire God, He will enlarge our capacity for more of Him.

My prayer is that you will experience God in ways that you never have before. Yes, my friend there is a place for you by God. We are under an open heaven and you will experience the rain of His presence and the rain of His anointing.

Blessed are they that hunger and thirst after righteousness for they shall be filled (St Matthew 5:6).

1 Samuel 15:22

"And Samuel said, Hath the Lord as great delight in burnt offerings and sacrifices, as in obeying the vice of the lord? Behold, to obey is better that sacrifice, and to hearken than the fat of rams."

CHAPTER TWENTY-EIGHT
LIFE AND LEGACY

Life is what you live but a legacy is what you leave behind. My life has been influenced by great men and women who have lived exemplary lives before me and have left me a legacy of prayer, intercession, perseverance and faith.

I know without a doubt that God plants people in our lives to be signposts, mentors, and examples in this journey called life. I have been mentored by a few people from a distance. They never knew I was gleaning from their lives but I learnt life lessons from their strengths and weaknesses. Some of them are deceased but they have left me a legacy and a few are living and their strength of character and tenacity has spoken volumes.

Shortly after I committed my life to Christ, a lady gave me this tract titled 'Others may, You Cannot'. I have held on this tract for a number of years, it has helped to mold and shape me into the person I am today. What a privilege it is to be able to share those words today.

> 'If God has called you to be really like Jesus He will draw you into a life of crucifixion and humility. God's call will put such demands of obedience on

you that you will not be able to follow other people or measure yourself by other Christians. At times, He will let other people do things which He will not let you do.

Other Christians who seem very religious will push themselves, pull wires, and work schemes to carry out their plans. You cannot, and if you attempt it, you will meet with failure and rebuke from the Lord.

Others may boast of themselves, of their work, of their successes, but the Holy Spirit will not allow you to do any such thing, and if you begin it, He will lead you to despise yourself and all your good works.

Others may be allowed to succeed in making money, or may have a legacy left to them, but it is likely God will keep you poor, God wants you to have something far better than gold, namely, a helpless dependence upon Him, that He may demonstrate His faithful love for you in supplying your needs day by day.

God may let others be honored and put forward, and keep you hidden in obscurity in order to produce some fragrant fruit for His coming glory which can only be produced in the shade. He may let others be great, but keep you small. He may let others do a work for Him and get the credit for it now. The reward for your work is held in the hands of Jesus, and you will not see it until He comes.

The Holy Spirit will put a strict watch over you with a jealous love. He will rebuke you for the little words and feelings or for wasting your time. So make up your mind that God is an infinite Sovereign and Has a right to do as He pleases with His own. He does not owe you an explanation of these mysteries. But if you give yourself to be His child, He will wrap you in a jealous love, and give you the precious blessings for those who belong, heart and soul, to Him.

Settle it forever, then, that you are to deal directly with the Holy Spirit, It is His option to tie your tongue, or chain your hand, or close your eyes in ways that He does not seem to use with others. And when you are so possessed by the living God that your heart delights over this peculiar, personal, private, jealous guardianship and management of the Holy Spirit over your life, you will have found the vestibule of Heaven'.

No. 76 Faith,
Prayer & Tract League 1

I also want to share another tract that was given to me years ago by a lady that has transitioned to glory. This one helped to develop me as an intercessor, it is entitled 'What it Means to Pray Through'.

Sister Dabney is a sister who makes prayer a business. If she sleeps at all, it is to be refreshed to resume her day and night vigils of prayer and waiting on God. She confines herself to one simple meal a day. She never has light conversation with anyone. Usually she comes quietly to a meeting an hour before the time announced and begins to pray. When the meeting is over she slips quietly to her room where her real ministry of travail for the deliverance of souls is carried on, far into the night.

In an interview Sister Dabney revealed how she came to enter this effective work for God and for souls. Her husband was a preacher. He was sent from a prosperous church in Philadelphia to labor in a poor one. At their first meeting no one was present but themselves. She saw it was going to be a difficult field for it was in the most wicked part of the city. She was made to know that nothing but prayer would touch the situation. She determined to give herself to prayer. She made a vow to God that if He would send sinners to that place and save them, she would give herself to prayer three days and three nights each week in the church for three years. She vowed during two of these years to fast as well as pray. When she first told her husband of her intentions, he was unwilling to have her spend three days and nights each week in the mission alone in prayer. But the Lord made Him to know it was of Him.

As soon as this little wife began to pray alone in her husband's mission, God began to work. Sinners were sent in and soon their hall was crowded out. Her husband asked her to pray for a larger place, God moved a merchant out of a better and larger building across the street and gave them this building. As Sister Dabney continued to pray, this building too was crowded out. Again her husband asked her to pray for a larger church. She did, and God gave them a fine large church on a main boulevard in the same neighborhood. Always the meetings were packed out and souls were delivered from sin and believers in multitudes were baptized in the Spirit.

One morning at the church door as she was entering to keep her vow of prayer, the Lord met her and said, "Go Home." But she did not want to go home. She wanted to pray. Then He asked her if she knew what day it was. She felt led to open her purse and read her vow and discovered from the date on the vow that she had exactly completed the three years she had given to God for prayer. She wanted to go into the church and adore and worship Him but He said again, "Go Home."

She obeyed. Her soul was exulting in His presence, Then He said to her, "Go to the basement." She was afraid of the dark basement and hesitated. She said, "Lord if you are going to take me home to glory, first let me see my husband and son." She was afraid the Lord was going to take her home in the midst of all this rejoicing. But she put on perfectly new pumps and went to the basement. Instead of darkness it was filled with a wondrous light. Then the Lord spoke to her gain. He said, "You have prayed through. Now I have come to bless you."

From the ceiling a fountain seemed to pour forth living water. This water rose higher and higher until it engulfed her. The joy and the presence were so gloriously manifest to her that she began to dance. The Lord told her that wherever she went and prayed, He would deliver sinners from their sins and fill believers with the Holy Spirit. She danced the heels and toes off her brand-new pumps.

This happened several years ago, and God has kept His word. Wherever Sister Dabney goes and gives herself to prayer, sinners are delivered and the saints are filled with the Holy Ghost and fire. She does not preach but only counsel saints and sinners to seek the Lord till He is found. The following letters give an intimate insight into her life of prevailing prayer:

I am burdened unto death this morning. My heart seems as if it were going to break. The burden of sinners is upon me greater than ever before. I can hear the cries of the dying world day and night.

"The Spirit is crying for a great outpouring of the Holy Ghost. This God's great ingathering day. For some cause He counted me worthy to suffer the agony of death that our poor people might be delivered before the cry is made, 'Behold, the Bridegroom is here!"

"There are few people who are willing to suffer that others might see the light. This is an awful day. The people are hungry for real examples of true holiness. The day is crowded with self and desire for personal gain, therefore we who are awakened must work double time to help push this battle to the gates."

"Prayer is the only remedy for this day of ills and chills. In the midst of it all, thank God I have found a place, away out in the Spirit upon the mountain, where a praying woman can go and be with God."

FREE TRACT SOCIETY 2

May you be blessed and challenged from reading how God used this preacher's wife and blessed her for her faithfulness. Prayer is work but it sure enough works. God has called us believers to pray without ceasing, and Sister Dabney has shown us what intercession is all about and the results of intercession.

This is just a portion of the tract as it is lengthy, however I have shared it because it set my spirit afire and opened my eyes deeply to what it means 'to pray through'.

CHAPTER TWENTY-NINE
OBEDIENCE

I believe it is most fitting that I conclude this book with a chapter on obedience. It is significant that we obey God when He gives us instructions, even when those instructions from a human point of view, do not make sense in the natural.

Sometime ago I heard Pastor Rod Parsley say this, 'When a word from God is given – reason is not required, faith alone must answer that door'. When God speaks, we must act in faith, even though we do not always comprehend the instructions. As you learn to walk in obedience, a word or a promise from God can become like a balm to your soul.

There was a time God spoke and I hesitated for a second but then I obeyed. I did not know how far reaching the act of obedience would go, nor did I know what the outcome would be until the next day when I received information regarding the situation. That was when I understood why I was given that instruction the day before. I truly thank God I obeyed His voice. God is always ahead of us and we must continue to send our prayers on up ahead. God is already there before we get there. Even as I type, I bow my spirit *'To the only wise God our Savior, be glory and majesty, dominion and power, both now and ever. Amen'*. (Jude 1:25).

Our God is all wise and He would not direct us to do certain things or to go places that are out of our comfort zone for naught. God always has a purpose and a plan for everything. God prompts and positions us to fulfill destiny so whatever God mandates for you to do, do it even if you cannot fathom the outcome. Obedience may take us into the unfamiliar; however, *'Behold, to obey is better than sacrifice, and to hearken than the fat of rams'* (1 Samuel 15:22b). Obedience will cause you to hear a word from God in season. The instructions may sound strange but can lead you right into the fulfillment of God's promise.

Years ago, when I was purchasing my first home, I had put down a finder's fee. After a month I was told to come and collect my money as someone else who had more money than I had purchased the home. Yes, to say I was disappointed is an understatement. Nevertheless, the Holy Spirit instructed me not to release the house out of my spirit and that if I did I would never get it. That period, the Lord encouraged me in prayer. He would show me my children playing out on the lawn and walking up and down the steps, but in the natural the twins could not walk as they were only weeks old. I recognized God was strengthening me to hold on, by showing me my future. More than once, God would use this vision to keep me encouraged because when we focus on what looks impossible, the devil will change our strengths into weaknesses to defeat us. So I had to redirect my focus in the word and let faith help me to hold on no matter what it looked like.

Approximately six months later, I went to the bank and a lady came up to me who I had only seen once, yet I recognized her. She asked me my name and she said she has been trying to find me; she inquired if I was still interested in purchasing her house. I told her yes, but they had told me the house was sold. She then said the deal fell through and she advised that I go to another agent that she had placed her property so we made an appointment. God instructed me to ask the loan officer to ask the seller to reduce the cost of the home I was interested in buying. He told me he could not do that as the owner was purchasing a new home and needed all the money.

I was impressed to push him to do it nevertheless. He finally agreed, more or less to appease me, but I knew he was just going through the motions. I never told him how much I wanted her to reduce the price. That night in prayer I did talk to God and I asked that the seller decrease the cost of the home by ten thousand dollars. All night in my sleep, it seemed every time I turned over, I thanked God for the answer.

The next day I was anxious to call the office, however the Holy Spirit instructed me not to call until 11:00 am. I went to the phone close to the time, but once again I was prompted to wait. When the clock finally struck 11:00 a.m. and I made the call, the loan officer excitedly told me that I would not believe the outcome. She had decreased the cost of the house by yes you guessed right, ten thousand dollars. Faithful is our God!

I remember my conversation with God when He first told me to believe for the house when it had been sold. I had the audacity to tell Him that if people knew I was believing Him for something that is in someone else's hands, they would think I was crazy. The Father lovingly responded to my audacious words by telling me, 'it is none of their business, all I need you to do is to trust me'. This was the time I learned to surrender the outcome to God. God does not play games with us or lead us down a yellow brick road, God is intentional, and He does fight our battles. However, we must obey him no matter what it looks like. God does not waste a life, nor does He waste suffering or a season.

Delays teach us wisdom. I can end this book with 'But God'. The word 'but' is a conjunction, and but changes a statement and erases what comes before. You have journeyed with me as I have had to lay down beside still waters and allow God to restore my soul through experiences that have fortified me and made me stronger, wiser and developed my faith.

And there have been other times I have walked through the valley of the shadow of death as I have suffered losses of all kinds. 'But God' has always been by my side, leading me, feeding me and instructing me.

There have been seasons of mourning, but like Rizpah, my season and your season of mourning will not go unnoticed. Rizpah's season of mourning was honored by the King and he gave her sons a proper burial (2 Samuel 21:14).

Our King, the King of Kings has been faithful and in response to His faithfulness, we say 'But God'!

CONCLUSION

The prophet Isaiah personified Israel in the female gender, when he challenged a barren woman to sing. *'Sing! O barren, thou that didst not bear; break forth into singing, and cry aloud, thou that didst not travail with child; for more are the children of the desolate than the children of the married wife, saith the Lord* (Isaiah 54:1).

Isaiah was prophesying Israel's future. Isaiah paints a beautiful picture of restoration when Israel's suffering and trials would come to an end. He shows them what the future will look like by using the analogy of a barren woman. Spiritual barrenness can render us ineffective in God's service, if we wallow in the past. However, as you thirst for more of Him, your barrenness will give way to fruitfulness. The above text has meant a lot to me over the years and has sustained me as I have proven God to restore.

The loss of a relationship can leave you forlorn and barren. In spite of this, I was determined that divorce would not render me a barren woman. Long before my marital status changed, I fervently pursued God from the time I was in my teens. There has always been a hunger and a thirst for the deeper things of God. I was intentional for the Lord to enlarge my territory. God placed me in many positions and places to make deposits in people from all walks of life. I was most satisfied when I would be about my Father's business unaware that God was enlarging my territory.

I have had many experiences where the enemy tried to break my spirit, but I fought back to remain steadfast and unbroken. The hunger and thirst I had for God sustained me and kept me going. The Holy Spirit led me and fed me. I was being prepared for the years of heartache and pain that in time encroached upon me. God had given me a reservoir not only to sustain me, but for every hungry and thirsty soul He permitted to cross my path. *'And thou shalt be like a watered garden, and like a spring of water whose waters fail not* (Isaiah 58:11).

Water is a natural requisite for the human body, without it we would die. The body knows when it needs the intake of water, and our spirit knows when it is thirsty for the living God and there is no substitute for this longing. We must become like David in his quest for God. *'As the hart panteth after the water brooks, so panteth my soul after thee, O God* (Psalm 42:1).

Jesus thirsted on the cross, He asked for water, but instead, they gave him vinegar to drink. I can't even imagine what He went through, but He endured so that we would drink of the living water.

Are you thirsty enough to pursue after the only one that can offer you living water? *'For I will pour water upon him that is thirsty, and floods upon the dry ground'* (Isaiah 44:3a).

Just as water is essential to the physical body, we need the living water that Jesus offered the Samaritan woman at the well. Jesus asked the woman to give Him a drink and she responded with a question, *'Why are you asking me a woman of Samaria for water – as the Jews have no dealings with the Samaritans'* (John 4:9). Jesus answered and said unto her, *If thou knewest the gift of God, and who it is that saith to thee, Give me to drink, thou wouldest have asked of Him, and He would have given thee living water* (John 4:10).

Jesus initially asked the woman a question to facilitate learning and to prepare her for the water He had to offer. There are times in the

Bible that Jesus asked a symbolic question to raise the individual's level of awareness and help them to address the situation. At times God will ask us questions so that we can see things from His perspective, then we are able to confront them.

Evaluate your spiritual appetite; How hungry and thirsty are you? Are you satisfied or are you hungry for more? I encourage you to chase the glory. As God ministers to you and fills you up, you are able to live in the overflow and feed the hungry in spirit.

As I am writing the final pages of this book, I pray your spiritual appetite has been whetted and you are hungry for more.

Indeed, *'Deep calls unto deep at the noise of the waterspouts: all thy waves and thy billows are gone over me'* (Psalm 42:7). The deep place in you touches the deep place in God. Get ready for the deluge!

'Blessed are they which do hunger and thirst after righteousness for they shall be filled' (Matthew 5:6).

EPILOGUE

Most of us have experienced feeling very thirsty on a summer's day and not having water within reach. And by the time water became available, you tilt your head back and take a long drink without pausing for seconds. You do not stop until your thirst has been quenched. Absolutely nothing else can satisfy our thirst like a tall glass of water. This should mirror of our thirst for God and our eagerness to constantly drink huge draughts from His wells.

There are twenty-four hours in a day, how you spend your day is your decision. If you want more of something, only you can make the time to pursue it. The enemy of our soul competes for our time and attention. He works hard to draw us away from the things of God. Sometimes we have a fight on our hands to spend quality time with God, because legitimate things demand our time and attention. However, it is up to us to schedule in time that counts.

We are challenged on a daily basis; therefore, our time with God has to be a discipline. Jesus is our example. If you keep hungering and thirsting after God – that hunger and thirst will cause you to pursue the presence of the Lord. The Holy Spirit finds us where we are and as He ministers to our spirit – lifts us up where we belong. Jesus is a rock in a weary land and a shelter in the time of storm (GIA Publications).

When the presence of the Lord overtakes you, you are caught up in the wonder of who God is. The floodgates of heaven opens and He rains down on you. Worship becomes spontaneous, it flows out of you like water from a fountain or rain from heaven. It is natural and all you want to do is worship, worship and adore Him. As the Holy Spirit woos you, God the Father draws you into His presence and you become so filled with gratitude to the King of Kings and the Lord of Lords, out of you will flow an exuberant praise.

As you wait, and the presence of God floods your soul, scales begin to fall off your eyes, what was demanding your time and attention pales in the presence of the Lord. There is a peace that hoovers over you, what may have been weighing you down begins to lift and the burden gets lighter when you are in the presence of the King.

When we are hungry, we eat until we are satisfied! Do not allow the enemy to steal your spiritual appetite, as long as you are hungry you shall be filled. Keith Staten's song describes the sentiment of my heart, 'Lord I thirst for you, I long to be in your presence, my soul shall wait for you, Father draw me nearer, draw me nearer to the beauty of your holiness'.

As long as you have a hunger and a thirst for God you will keep panting after him. Beware of the things that will draw you away rather than draw you to God.

When worship becomes a lifestyle, you will fulfill the text that says, *'Sing forth the honor of His name: make His praise glorious* (Psalm 66:2). As we seek to honor God in word and deed our relationship with Him deepens and He is honored in our lifestyle of continuous worship and hungering for Him.

When David was in the wilderness of Judah, he expressed himself to God in this manner, *'O God, thou art my God; early will I seek thee; my soul thirsteth for thee, my flesh longeth for thee in a dry and thirsty land, where no water is'* (Psalm 63:1). Every believer should pray as David did in this Psalm. It describes a man's deep longing in his heart for God, one that can only be satisfied by an intimate relationship with Him (footnotes from The Full Life Study Bible, note (1) page 856).

It has been said, 'it takes twenty-one days to form a habit'. Perhaps you can read one chapter a day for the next twenty-seven days and be intentional in your quest of seeking God. Your goal is to really get to know God in a new way as you learn to enjoy and soak in His presence. I suggest you journal each day, every day will be different. Highlight what you gleaned, learned, even heard or experienced.

'Hungering for God' is intended to draw you into a closer walk with God and in spite of the anomalies of life, you will let nothing stop you from pursuing the lover of your soul.

HUNGERING FOR GOD

I created man with a thirst and a hunger for me
Many override this desire just content to 'be'
They fill that empty chamber with whatever satisfies
Drugs, alcohol, perversion; causing them to deny
I alone can answer their heart's cry.

I send my word using every available tool
Content for a while they obey the golden rule
I offer repentance you deny me like a fool.
I am a jealous God, they must return to me
Salvation is the answer, I can set them free

David the psalmist an example for all to know
His sin with Bathsheba caused him a blow
He repented and cried out for mercy
I forgave him and made him worthy
Yesterday's sin became a memory.

Prayer is an opportunity to fill yourself with me
I long to fill your thirsty soul as deep as the sea

I filled you with my treasure without measure

I want you to do more than survive

I offer you my presence; it will keep you alive.

As you surrender I offer sweet release

Part time communication must cease

I satisfy your soul with my peace

I invite you to come and sit at my feet

Thriving in victory is definitely the key.

By Pastor Yvonne Ramsay

NOTES

Chapter 26 – Life and Legacy

1. **Others May. You Cannot**. No. 76 Faith, Prayer and Tract League, Grand Rapids, Michigan, 49504-1390

2. **What It Means to Pray Through,** FREE TRACT SOCIETY, 2408 W. 7th S. Los Angeles, CA 90057.

ABOUT THE AUTHOR

Rev. Dr. Yvonne I. Ramsay has been serving the Lord for 50 years and is the founding Pastor of Breath of Life Ministries. She is a Marriage and Family Counselor. She obtained a Master of Arts degree at Briercrest Biblical Seminary in Canada in 2003. In 2015 she received an 'Honorary' Doctorate of Divinity from CICA International University and Seminary'. She is the author of 'Come Forth and Fly'.

She is the mother of D'Vonne, Jereme, and Jaime Ramsay. Also, grandmother of Jamie Madison and Xavier Levi T. Ramsay.

Her personal philosophy of counselling ministry can be found in the words of Henry Nouwen, "Just as bread needs to be broken to be given, so do our lives. It is from her own life experiences she is always ready to give.

She has counseled, mentored, and ministered to both men and women for nearly forty years. She has compassion for those that are broken hearted, hurting and helpless – assisting them to reauthor a new story of their preferred reality as well as ministering to their spiritual needs through the power of the Holy Spirit.

Rev. Yvonne has served in many capacities within the church, but prayer is her passion as she intercedes for the lost. Her ministry is born out of her relationship with God.

Email: pastorbreathoflifemin@gmail.com

www.ingramcontent.com/pod-product-compliance
Lightning Source LLC
Chambersburg PA
CBHW071007160426
43193CB00012B/1960